TRY, CATCH

TRY, CATCH

BY DAVID CANTÚ

NEW DEGREE PRESS

TRY, CATCH

ISBN 978-1-63676-533-4 *Paperback*
      978-1-63676-077-3 *Kindle Ebook*
      978-1-63676-078-0 *Ebook*

CONTENTS

———

ACKNOWLEDGMENTS

——

I want to thank everybody who contributed to my campaign and who have been supporting me for the past six months. This book would not have been made without you.

Colin Abel, Jeffrey Arango, Ahmad Attia, Diane Bahrenburg, Steven Birmingham, Rolando Bonachea, Alejandra Brambila, Francisco Brambila, Ezra Brooks, Gary Burdette, McKay Burdette, Renato Cantú, Karla Cantú, Lorena Brambila Cantú, Cecy Cantú, Manuel Ortiz Chavez, Patricio Criollos, Remigio Arenas Muñoz de Cote, Sofía Margarita Lozano de la Garza, Surya Dhir, Sergio Díaz, Emily Elenio, Andrew Gaffney, Mauricio Valdés Galán, Antonio Garza, Hernán Garza, Gerardo Treviño Garza, Marco Gaspari, Carlos Gil, Eduardo Villanueva González, Juan Cantú Guajardo, Paul Harryhill, Tan Huynh, David Izek Jakubowicz, Joseph Kelleher, Eric Koester, Marta Kozlowska, Daniel Kutzin, Brian Li, Lorena Martinez Lombard, Zander G Lopez, Dylan Love, Alicia Lu, Alexander M Lyons, Sagid Manriquez, Mikael Mantis, Aaron Mittleman, Chris Motz, Romin Parekh, Jonah Peter, Arun Ponnusamy, Martin Popov, Roberto Quintanilla, Kashyap Rajagopal, Juan Manuel Ramírez, Pablo Redondo, Dylan Reim, Geoff Rosin,

Diego Sada, Javier Sagastuy, Ken Chanseau Saint-Germain, Hannah Salazar, Andres Salinas, Tomás Sánchez, Adrian Serna, Jiyoung Song, Mario Trivella, Surya Vijayaraghavan, Isabella Viney, Generoso Cantú Westendarp, Ivan Zambrano, Daniel Zambrano

I also want to thank New Degree Press staff and my editors for their guidance and advice throughout the way.

To flowers, who still continue to blossom in even the darkest of years.

And to my parents, family, and friends. I guess you guys are important too.

1.

"Excuse me, excuse me..."

A man wearing pants tucked into a pair of bright, colorful socks, each a different color, palette, and style, rushed past John Buntington down the long and sinuous stairway to the waiting area of 22nd Street Station. John was instantly impressed at the man's ability to carry a worn-out, upside-down scooter on his shoulder, avoiding other commuters who might not be as awake as he was. It was, after all, 6:45 in the morning.

John himself carefully took each step down the staircase covered with morning dew, actively trying not to slip. He did not want to show up to his first day of work with a muddied outfit.

The scooter man got to the bottom of the stairs and briskly walked to a very specific and seemingly random location on the extensive, rocky waiting area, folded up his scooter, and rested it standing up against a big concrete pillar.

What's his deal?

John got to the platform and stood some forty feet away from the scooter man. The train would not be coming for another fifteen minutes, but, just as he did not want to show up with a muddied outfit, he did not want to be late. He had read somewhere at some point in his life that first impressions are everything, although he wasn't able to recall exactly where or when he read that. It might have just been his dad in one of the countless and unsolicited advice calls he sometimes received.

Today was the day. It had been a long time coming. Finally, the promise given by the many years of education was coming to fruition. He was on his way to his very first day of work as an adult, as a graduate, as an engineer. It was the first day of the rest of his life, as they say. He joined millions of other Americans who look for happiness, money, and fulfillment. On paper, John had always known that getting all three was not a simple task. But he had repeatedly been told throughout his relatively short life by society that if he followed the pattern that his parents took, and did as he's supposed to do, he'd have at least a decent shot at achieving those goals.

He found that, in reality, it was much, much harder than anyone had ever promised him. After all, he had been training the past four years, attending college for the moment where he no longer paid an institution to write code, but rather, he would be the one getting paid by an institution to do so. Paid a lot, in fact. More than he deserved, but that really didn't bother him. If everyone else was making that much money, why couldn't he?

All throughout college, he struggled to balance his social life and the ridiculous amounts of work assigned by professors who, in his mind, were truly out to get him and the rest of the students.

Did I really need to do three problem sets a week? I mean, come on. Three? Monday, Wednesday, and Friday?

Or, more likely, those professors valued the cost of tuition at his college and wanted to make sure he got what he paid for, or what the bank who loaned him money paid for. That was always the more likely explanation but certainly not the most enthralling.

He would go straight home from the Engineering Quad, drop off his backpack, take a quick shower, slap some deodorant on his armpits and some gel on his hair, and go out to the local college bar. He had a good time with his friends when he went out, although he didn't consider the collegiate bar scene his scene. But then again, no one would dare admit that the collegiate bar scene was their scene. He got drunk some nights and went home to "pull trig" as his friends used to say.

Some other nights he would merely have a couple of beers or drinks but only with the goal of convincing his actually drunk friends to go with him to get late-night food, like burgers, pizza, or even chicken wings. John not only looked forward to the food but the occasional fight that would break out at two in the morning in these establishments.

Free entertainment.

"I'm so drunk, bro, I need some of that good, good shit," he would say in a voice that wasn't really his, but everyone who ever walked out of a bar at night in a college would always pretend to have. More often than not he would succeed in his goal and would end up back home consuming the food without saying a word to his companion. That meant a good night was had.

When it was all said and done, four years of his youth had gone by. Friendships, girlfriends, a high GPA, self-respect, mild depression, self-loathing, physical fitness, food habits, and philosophical tendencies had all come and gone. Now was the time to enter the so-called and feared "real world" that his parents and teachers had insisted, from as long as he can remember until he had his college diploma in his hand, he was not, and could never be, ready for.

At this particular point in time, standing on the train station, waiting to start his commute to work, John Buntington thought of his old friend Karl Marx, and how he thought of himself as a Communist. However, he also thought of himself as a hypocrite, as he was fully aware that he was going into corporate America. He didn't care too much, though. He had done his part.

Born and raised in a small town in Indiana to a family of corn farmers, John didn't really have high aspirations for himself, and neither did his parents, his younger sister, his three-legged dog Triad, or the hundreds of acres of corn that year in and year out were a constant reminder of how cyclical life was. You work the soil at the beginning of the season, plant the seed, and if you do everything just as you're supposed to corn would come out the other end. John was well on his way to becoming a beautiful, ripe, yellow corn.

Except he never really wanted to do anything with corn ever in his life. He was a proud flour tortilla man, and intended to keep it that way until the day he died.

Studying Computer Science had always been his first choice, ever since he had read the average salary of graduating students in engineering was the highest for those going into Software Engineering. However, this conclusion did not come without the constant reminders from his dad, his mom, his extended family that all that "computer junk" wasn't going to get him anywhere.

At points he even imagined his three-legged dog also lecturing him.

"Sure," his dad would say, "they'll pay you enough to keep you happy, but in a couple of years that will stop, the bubble will burst, and you'll come crawling back home to work on God's given gift to the world."

"Okay, Dad," he would answer every time.

The train ride to South Bay would take approximately an hour a day, which was alright by him.

A loud horn blasted through the tunnel leading up to the station, snapping John out of his rumination. He was made aware of his surroundings again as the train pulled up to the platform. At least a hundred people had arrived at the station without John noticing and were all lining up in particular spots, just like the scooter man had—who, by the way, was now at the front of a line.

John walked over and lined up behind the rest of the commuters. The train slowed down to a stop, its doors opened, and people trickled in.

He took that step into the train and felt like a new man. He was on his way to work.

However, this feeling quickly subsided as he realized there were no available seats for him to sit and stare out the window, thinking about his past, present, and future. He would have to do so standing up, rubbing up against an old lady reading a newspaper in a language that was not English. Perhaps Russian.

He spotted the scooter man sitting comfortably in a window seat.

He knows what he's doing.

John took a hold of a steel bar and resumed his thinking. That Monday morning, his first day on the train, he didn't listen to any music or podcasts, or even try to read the paper or whatever people do on a commute ride. He looked outside, although through a small gap in the passengers, and imagined himself in a movie, registering all the different landscapes shown to him through this window.

Leaving San Francisco, the industrial nature of South San Francisco came into view; all the scrapyards, big factories, abandoned buildings, and railroads, as well as small houses close to the train tracks juxtaposed with the big, beautiful houses up in the hills. He hoped one day he would be able to wake up in a house up in those hills, look out to the Bay, and again, pretend to be in a movie, maybe even the same movie, one that's excessively long for no good reason and shows a relatively boring coming-of-age story. Millbrae's station, on the other hand, was techy and advanced. Tall structures with tracks coming in from all angles, people transferring from one train to another, commuting like commuters do.

The next stop was Redwood City.

Much different than San Francisco.

Didn't necessarily look like a city, compared to where he went to school, but it sure looked like a metropolis compared to "Small Town," Indiana.

The train came to a sudden stop, and John, who had let go of the steel bar, almost toppled the old lady over. She was getting off at that station, along with about half of the other passengers. He remembered his first time in New York City, where, thinking he had control over the subway's brisk starts and stops, he had tripped and fallen into a musician playing for tips. The alto sax he played was broken, and John had almost gotten beaten up. He did get shamed by the rest of the passengers on the Q train. Enough for him to always hang on to things in trains. Well, almost always.

He sat down on a freed-up spot.

He was truly amazed at the diversity of people in the train. The excitement for finding a diverse, fulfilling atmosphere at work built in him, stop after stop. Palo Alto was up next, and by God, was it beautiful. An awful lot of land was not really being used. He thought back to other neighborhoods that the train had already passed and how cramped and dirty they seemed to be compared to Stanford.

Oh, well, at least anyone can come visit, at least those who can afford the non-negligible train fee.

Hospital workers, students, and some tech people were the passengers John assumed got off the station there, waiting on *The Marguerite* to take them to their respective places.

Mountain View was as uneventful as he had thought and, by that point, most of the people had gotten off. All of a sudden, John looked around and realized he was the last person on the train, alongside the scooter man. The feeling of a community of workers and people commuting vanished, and he suddenly felt alone and scared. Luckily for him, after what seemed like an eternity but in reality was only around fifteen minutes, the train arrived at San Jose, his stop and the train's final destination.

He stood up, put on his backpack, tightened the straps, and walked out of the train with a giant grin on his face. San Jose Diridon was not like the other stations, in the sense that this was the first stop that actually looked like one and not some dingy gazebo by the tracks.

He went down the stairs to get to a tunnel that would eventually lead him out to the main hall. From there, it was only about a fifteen to twenty-minute walk to his office, which was downtown. It did not seem like Redwood City, Palo Alto, or even Mountain View. San Jose was separate from the rest of the Bay. More space, fewer buildings. He started his strut, chin up and eyes focused on the horizon. He had worked for this; he was ready.

"Watch out!"

He turned around quickly and lightly bumped into someone riding an electric scooter. His heart skipped a beat, and he almost fell to the ground. It was the scooter man.

"Hey, watch where you're walking, buddy! You're gonna get yourself killed. Can't you see that I'm trying to scoot over here!" the man said, as he scooted away toward downtown.

John, confused and shocked, assessed his surroundings to make sure there were no more imminent attacks.

Okay, I'm definitely on a sidewalk, which I'm pretty sure should not have these sorts of scooters.

Then he started to see them everywhere. The scooters. So many scooters. There was one every fifteen feet or so. Some were standing up on their legs, some were on the ground, as if they had given up on life and had decided to take a nap. He was mesmerized by them, and it took someone tapping him on the shoulder to break him out of it.

"John?! I saw what happened to you. Are you okay? I'm not sure if you remember me, but I'm on your team. I believe I was one of the people to interview you?"

"Hey, yeah, sorry. I don't know what happened there. Some guy came out of nowhere riding this thing, and he hit me on the side. Suresh, right?"

"Yeah, man, I'm Suresh! Well, welcome to San Jose, one of the friendliest cities in America!" he said, and his laugh had a hint of sadness in it.

"I can already tell."

They continued chatting during their walk, discussing all the banal things people who don't really know each other discuss. *How is your new apartment? How was the end of your schooling? How's living up in the city? Expensive? I bet it is, everything here is so expensive. Are you excited for your first day at work? You must be! It's a great company to work for. How was your commute? Do you have roommates? How are they?*

John was happy to answer the incessant questions, but quickly got bored with them.

Then he spotted what appeared to be feces on the road. "Is that shit?" he asked Suresh, pointing to it.

"Where? That green bag?"

"Yeah, that one."

"Yeah, that is human shit. Sometimes these poor guys don't have anywhere to go, so they just go where they can. Can't really blame them."

There were many tents populated by people all throughout their walk to the office. The tents frequently had some sort of mattress or bed, as well as bicycle or at least bicycle parts. John was confused.

People just walk past these guys every day?

"Yeah, I mean, there are some public bathrooms too," continued Suresh. "I think there's one a couple of miles away they can use. Again, absolutely *terrible* situation. I wish the city would do more."

"Yeah, you're right."

They got to the lobby where a committee of enthusiastic people were greeting the new employees. Balloons and free food for everyone.

"Do you want coffee?" asked Suresh before he joined the rest of the people starting their work today.

"No, I'm okay. I don't really drink coffee."

"You will soon. Welcome to Corporate America, my friend." Suresh walked into the building.

"Welcome to the company!" yelled one of the people attending the new employees. "We are so excited to have you and cannot wait for you guys to have an impactful and meaningful contribution to the company. The best lies ahead!"

I hope she's not lying ahead of time.

John sat down at a table and waited for orientation to begin.

2.

The first couple of weeks at work had passed, and it was time for John's weekly pre-scheduled meeting with his manager.

The first one had gone okay. John had learned most of the team's dynamics. He and Adi had come to an understanding of how their relationship would work. Mostly the basics: how he liked to get feedback and praise, and the sort of areas that John was looking to improve and focus on during his time under him. Adi had done most of the talking.

John wasn't sure there would be enough to talk about with Adi every single week, but for now, there seemed to be enough content to power through.

Apart from that meeting, John was having a hard time figuring out Adi and what his managerial style was. In their first demo meeting, Adi had not quite acted how he had presented himself to be in their first meeting, often interrupting people and repeating others' words as his own.

This was John's first job, so he did not have a point of reference on how a manager should act versus how he himself should behave. To John's own amusement, Adi, at this point, was simultaneously both the best and worst manager he'd ever had.

Suresh would pop by his desk all the time and ask him how he was doing or if he needed any help, while Nirmala, one of the other engineers on the team, seemed to mostly keep to herself. She would occasionally join in to talk to John, but usually kept busy at her desk. And from what John could tell after the first round of demos that morning, she was a software engineering force to be reckoned with, unlike Suresh, who had said that the "demo gods" were not on his side that day.

John put that one in his back pocket.

As he walked into Adi's office, John thought that maybe he should come into the meeting with a clear mind and listen to what his manager had to say. He had successfully convinced himself, despite Adi's poor showing that morning, that he should trust his manager. He had, after all, been in the industry longer than John had "been over five feet tall," as Adi had told him last week.

"John! Come in! Sit down, sit down!" said Adi as John walked into his tiny office.

The shelves in the room were crowded with old JavaScript books, a bottle of whiskey with a lonely cup next to it, and a good number of pictures of Adi with his family.

Adi liked to keep the shades down even though he had an excellent view of the street. However, John noticed that he wasn't the only one to keep them that way. As someone whose best office view consisted of a senior director's door and his own trash can, John envied them. Even though it had only been a couple of weeks, he already felt a slight resentment at their choice to be in the darkness.

He did manage to get a good look at the senior director's lunch every day and had even gotten inspiration on how to build some of his salads. The senior director was a busy man who had lunch meetings very often, or so it appeared that way. His computer monitor faced the other way, and John never really knew what he was (or was not) watching on there. One of the greatest mysteries of the world.

"Hey, Adi, what's up?"

"Hey, John," said Adi slowly as he began to close down the windows in his computer, which mostly consisted of You-Tube videos and email applications. John caught a glimpse of a video before it vanished titled *How to Deal With Young Engineers in Your Team - 101!*

Adi did not say anything as he finished closing up. This inability to talk and close down the windows reminded John of an assignment he once had for his hardware architecture class back in college, the main idea being that a processor can only process one instruction at a time.

I wonder how many cores he's running in his head.

"Hey, Adi?" Adi had not talked in a couple of seconds so John felt obligated to fill the silent room with his own voice.

"Hey, John, how are you? Good? Good. As you know, as a team, we have on-call. I wanted to talk to you about it. I think it's time for you to start being on the rotation. It's like becoming a man, bar mitzvah, as they say."

"Okay, sure, when would I start? And what exactly does it entail? I'm sorry, I'm just not very familiar with the process. I have some idea of what on-call means but really not much more than that."

"Um, I think the current shift ends at four, so I wanted you to take over after that."

"Oh, okay, is there some sort of training that I could look at or something?"

"There is...some. I'll send you the links later today if you want. But don't worry about it. There is not much going on. No one ever gets paged, and even if you do, it's simple stuff. Usually, you just have to restart a service, and it would be okay. Maybe sometimes something else."

"Something else? Should I be taking notes?"

"No, no, you should be fine. Everything is going to be okay. Our systems are very strong, as you know. They are as strong as the company stock. I made sure of that ever since I got here. Be happy, don't worry."

John winced. "Don't worry, be happy."

How can you disrespect the lyrics like that? Is he doing it on purpose?

"Be happy, don't worry," challenged Adi.

He can't be serious.

"I think it's 'don't worry, be happy.' It really doesn't matter."

The following day at 2:57 a.m.

John's ringtone sounded loudly. Startled and with a cheek wet with drool, he raised his hand and reached toward his phone. He didn't recognize the number on the screen.

He had forgotten he was on-call. John immediately recognized a strong headache coursing through his forehead.

Who in the fuck is this?

"Hello?" he said.

A bold, heavy, and excessively Eastern European accented voice punched him awake through the phone's speaker. "Hello, yes, am I speaking to John? John Boonting…Boontington? Did I say that right?" A short pause. "Who is this?"

"Yeah, this is John. Who are you again?"

Why the fuck is Putin calling me at this time?

And then it hit him. Hit him like Sputnik crashing down through the atmosphere, breaking through his ceiling and landing right on his drooled-damped face.

Ah, shit.

"Yes, John, this is Alexei with Worldwide Support. Sorry to wake you up. You are in United States, yes? There is incident that your system triggered. Your system is reporting much longer than average response times, and it is starting to impact other systems, so we were called to go find someone. So, I do my job and I looked up the list, and you are on-call. We need you to come help solve it or tell us what to do. These alarms are not stopping."

Alarms? Average response times?

"Oh, man, really?" John got out of bed and turned on his cheap LED Amazon-bestseller lamp that barely illuminated the room. "Let me get my computer and take a look." He had no clue how to solve the issue or even what the issue was. But he had a misguided confidence that a simple restart of the system would resolve the alarms and get the response times back to normal, whatever that meant.

The day before, in Adi's office

"I really thought it was be happy, don't worry," continued Adi. "Are you sure?"

"It literally doesn't matter."

"Anyway, like I said, everything should be okay."

"Got it, got it."

"Yes, so the way on-call works is we rotate through the team. Each person gets a week of on-call, and then gives report to the next person before the end of the week."

John stared blankly at him. Something gave him the impression that some weeks happened to be easier than others. He hoped in that instant that the Law of Averages would come to his rescue on his first week.

Adi continued, "Did we not put a section on it during the introductory video? Did we miss that? Can you add to it if we missed it?"

The introductory video did contain some details about what it meant to be on-call, narrated by the most senior engineer in the team, Dinh. Being on-call meant essentially being the team's personal babysitter for the week. If anything went wrong with any of the systems, the on-call person would take a look and resolve it to the best of their ability.

Another key responsibility John noted was that if anyone had any questions about the team's systems and products, no matter how easy and time wasting they were to answer, the on-call person would have to respond and educate them in a well-mannered way.

John forgot the rest.

"Okay, good, what time is that meeting today? I don't remember seeing it in my calendar."

"Today's meeting is…canceled, I think. Suresh had a dental appointment. But I don't think anything happened this week. I think you'll be okay. Don't worry, be happy, man!" he said with a big smile on his face and patted John on the shoulder. "Just remember to put your phone on loud."

John did so in that moment.

"Okay, done. Anything else you want to talk about?" He wanted to get out of there and back to trying get a sense for the systems he was going to be on the hook for.

"Yes, one more thing. What do you think so far of the team? Any inefficiencies you are seeing? Anything we can fix now? You have a fresh pair of eyes. Let's put them to use."

A bit too Hannibal Lecter-ish for my taste, but we'll let it slide.

John pondered for a second and looked around the room. He was trying hard to come up with something intelligent to say but could not do so. He had only been there a couple of weeks at most. He had no idea what an inefficient workspace was. He was, after all, an engineer and not a consultant.

That much, we know for sure.

A pair of running shoes with what appeared to be dirty socks lay in the corner of the room, which made John notice the other articles of clothing strewn throughout the office, such as a tie hanging from a book that stuck out of the bookshelf.

How long has this man worked here?

Then he said, "Yeah, as a matter of fact I have some questions about our schedule. Why do we have so many meetings? Last Wednesday we pretty much spent the entire day in meetings and didn't get anything done. Is that usually the case?"

"Not usually, no," Adi lied to himself and John. "Usually, we are done by two, and people can get back to work. We need all the meetings."

"Don't we have a planning meeting to be more prepared for planning itself?"

"Yes, we do. Very observant, John!"

This did not seem like the efficient and fun tech industry that he had read and learned so much about. John also understood that he was new to the team, and his criticism of the way things were being done in Adi's team was probably unfounded and he would promptly be, hopefully, proven incorrect.

"Why is that? It seems rather redundant."

"I agree, but the feedback from the team a couple of months ago was that we weren't planning properly and we weren't finishing sprint tasks because of that. So now, we are focusing more on the planning meeting for planning, so that when we show up to planning, we know what we are going to plan and come out of it prepared."

That was the longest sentence John had heard in a while. It bewildered him how he thought it made any sense.

"Makes sense to me," said John.

The following day at 3:15 a.m.

John joined the virtual Situation Room, as they were called, on the computer a couple of minutes after he first got the call. People would talk every couple of minutes and ask for updates from John.

The first thing he did was to try and restart the services to see if the latency-triggered alerts would calm down and go away.

"They're not going away," he said to the peanut gallery in the Situation Room, which involved a couple of guys from the now-identified Ukraine, and another American, whose service was being affected by John's.

Michael, the other American, said, "Well, is there some sort of runbook that you can take a look at? We're flying by the seat of our pants here, kid. I don't think that our system can handle your latency much longer. I mean, it can technically still respond, but we're customer-facing. We are the face of the product. We gotta fix this. We gotta."

"Yeah, John, can we help in any way?" asked one of the Ukrainians.

Be happy, don't worry, my ass.

John scrambled through the company's documents tagged with his team's flag to try to find the runbook that would help him fix the failures or at least mitigate them. After scrolling and skimming through many pages titled with acronyms he didn't understand or have any context for, like Project P.A.L.E. or Program S.H.I.N.E., he finally found something that looked relatively familiar.

He navigated into the page Apple F'd it to look for "intermittent." No result.

Fuck.

He then tried "failure," for which the navigator found fifty-five matches on the page. He went through every single one, with only the backlight of his computer hitting his face, and his neck arched. He was butt-naked, as he liked to sleep, and his computer sat on his crotch. At that point, he realized that it was heating up, so he put a pillow under it.

Balls are sweaty no more. Now I can get to work.

It wasn't until the fiftieth match that he found what he was looking for. The page read *Latency Alerts.*

Aha! Here it is.

"Let me try something else," said John, as he started to read the table to find out what steps he needed to take.

Alarm—The System is having a high latency and is experiencing longer than average response times. This may cause the dependencies to weaken and eventually crash. It is important that this problem is fixed as soon as it is found out. Some customer-facing products depend on this system.

Got it, what do I do?

Solution—Restart the System.

The day before, in Adi's office

"Okay, good! Good, John," said Adi, standing up. "Thanks for coming. Worst-case scenario, if any real problem happens while you're on-call, you can always call...call Suresh."

"Why Suresh?"

Although he knew the rest of his team to an okay degree, he was not quite comfortable yet to just call a second person to join him in case of an emergency. Besides, if the first demo was any indication, Suresh, or anyone else in the team for that matter, did not seem like the type of person who would want to be woken up in the middle of the night, or really any other point of the day, to go help out. Maybe they were, but John did not want to find out.

"He's the second in the on-call queue. He knows the system like the back of his hand. But don't call him unless you absolutely need to, which will never happen, because everything will be okay. But if it does, call him. But it won't. So don't call him. He doesn't like being woken up."

"So, should I call him?"

"You won't need to."

"Okay. Adi, I think I'm going to go back to my desk now and look up some stuff on my computer to try to learn at least the basic behavior of the system. I'm getting there but I need a little more time."

"Of course, of course, John. You are a responsible engineer! I like you already."

You hired me.

He went and looked up some documents to read. He placed each one in a separate tab and made a note to self of how important they were. Then, he went ahead and did absolutely nothing the rest of the day, which was about half an hour, except stare at some of his social media feeds.

The following day, 3:20 a.m.

"God fucking damn it," murmured John quietly enough so that the rest of the call couldn't hear him.

"Sorry, what did you say? I couldn't hear you," said Michael.

"Mr. Buntington," hopped in Alexei. "Do you need some assistance? I can offer you my assistance. I just need you to communicate with me what you need and how I can help."

John took the Ukrainian man's help and the two of them perused a lot of documents together, trying to figure out what the hell was wrong with the system. They were able to narrow down the problem to one system, John's team's system, the one causing the alert.

Useless.

"This is good!" said the Ukrainian man. "This means that it is a problem with your system and your system only, and that you can fix it. That's what this means. So now let us just do that and fix it."

"I said I'm going to try something else," said John.

John restarted the system one more time. And then again. And then one final time, until luckily enough, the alarms started going green and the system seemed to be behaving normally again. Latencies were starting to cool down, and response times were back to normal.

"I think it's working now," said Michael.

John sighed with relief. He could not believe how exhausted he was. His bed was calling him to sleep, and he was still naked.

"Alright, fellas, I think we should be good for the rest of the night. If anything, I'll check in the morning and make sure that things are running smoothly." John had no real intention of doing so.

"Good night, John Boontington."

They all hung up the call and left the Situation Room. John's phone vibrated one more time just as he connected it back to the charger. A message from Alexei Volkov: a simple emoji of a yellow smiley face with a military hat on doing a military salute.

John smiled and sent him one right back.

Although he had been annoyed, and very much so, at the fact that he was woken up in the middle of the night to deal with a problem that he was unprepared for, he had entered the night alone and left with a new friend, with whom he shared a feeling of comradery.

Alexei had been his partner in his very first Situation Room, the modern-day trenches. He had brought a sense of calm and anarchy all at the same time, while soothing him with his thick accent. John had not seen his face, nor did he want to look it up. All he knew was that some man halfway across the world had connected with him in a way he hadn't felt with anyone at his company yet.

Ah, it's not that big of a deal. Maybe I'm just tired.

John tended to get sentimental late at night.

After a quick visit to the bathroom, John laid in his bed, turned off the lamp, and checked his phone one last time. Part of him wanted to make sure he had not missed any calls or texts on his short trip to the bathroom but part of him wanted to take the phone and throw it out the window.

Nothing urgent, but he did find an email from his landlord, Jane.

Thursday 3:30 a.m.

Hey, all,

Friendly reminder to everyone that the trash is to be taken out BEFORE midnight and not after. Especially not at three in the morning.

Thanks,

Jane.

3.

One week later, 1:00 p.m., in the conference room

"How is everybody?" Adi asked his team, and thus began the meeting.

It was John's turn to give the on-call report to the team, where he would maybe get some deliverance for his troubles. They would get to know what they had put him through and knowing that fact gave him some solace. Maybe he would just find out that no one ever had a good time when they were on-call.

The silence in the room was not deafening. In fact, it was so silent that even old clever sayings did not apply. Everyone just stared at Adi as he smiled at his people, waiting for any sign of life.

"Well, good! I'm glad everyone is doing well! Let's get started!" said Adi.

He connected his computer to the HDMI cable, which projected his screen on the big monitors at the end of the room.

People were allowed to bring their laptops, so everyone was focused on those and not the newly projected screen. John was the only good student paying attention in class and not only because he was in the queue to present.

"There are three items we need to tackle today, team. On-call rotation, planning, and Adam and I have some important announcements to make," said Adi.

What about my on-call report?

John sat at one end of the table, the farthest away from his manager as possible, with his computer angled in such a way that no one would be able to see what he was 'working' on. To his own surprise, he had finished the on-call report before coming in to the meeting,

Maybe he forgot and we'll just do it at the end of the meeting. There is no way he'll forget something that is this important to me and the rest of the team.

He had given up on paying attention now that he knew there wasn't anything serious to talk about in the immediate future.

On a normal day, he would be scrolling through Twitter or looking at the table itself from the camera view provided by the video conferencing software. But today wasn't one of those days. Today, he sat there messaging people all through his team's extended organization trying to gain access to the necessary systems to get going on his main project led by Adam, the PM.

The project's name was Secure and Deliver, and John had no idea what it was about other than the fact that it had an absolutely moronic acronym. But that did not matter.

It kind of did matter, as he would eventually have to demo, but it didn't matter that much right now, and that's all that mattered. Things that were far away to John were sometimes almost invisible, if not fully transparent.

"So, we have bit of a problem," started Adi. "Next week is a holiday so we cannot just assign the whole week to someone because that is not fair. And as you all know, we are all about being fair in this team. Fair is good."

Everyone else seemed to know where Adi was going with this introductory statement. But again, no one looked and let him finish. John had not put the pieces of the puzzle together.

"I need volunteers for next week. We need to cover all days, as you guys know. Suresh? John? Amber? Any volunteers?" asked Adi, laying down the first cards on the table.

Everyone in the room immediately straightened up in their chairs and some of them put their elbows on the table. John felt a sudden air of animosity fill the room.

What is going on?

"Are we getting paid extra if we work that week?" asked Suresh, already knowing the answer to his question.

"I...don't think so? No, that budget has not been approved by my manager and is disagreed upon by the tech lead. And I disagree with both but you guys know how they are. They do not budge."

"Well, then why would anyone volunteer?" replied Suresh.

"Because it is your job."

And so, it officially began: the on-call poker. John had heard about it from Suresh in a team lunch at some point in the past couple of weeks. He didn't know much, but he did know that there would be no winners in this game, only people who would lose less.

Hamsters ran inside everybody's head as every engineer in the room tried to read each other's faces. John particularly noticed Dinh, who was systematically going through the team, one by one, looking them in the eye.

"I can't. I'm traveling, and I won't have service," said Dinh in a very final manner.

Really? No service at all? Fuck.

The first card had been played, and it was a powerful one. John supposed that once the "no service" card was played, it could only be played a couple of times more, at best, before it started to become suspicious. Dinh was a smart man for being the first one to play.

"I'm actually going to go get some coffee," Dinh said as he stood up and walked out of the room, everyone's eyes following his every move until the door shut behind his exit.

The bastard actually got away with it.

"Okay, anyone else?" asked Adi.

"I won't have service for a couple of days." Suresh tried his luck. A couple of days was a more reasonable and plausible amount of time to be out of service.

Is he bluffing?

"Which days?" replied Adi.

After a brief back and forth that had started with him negotiating being out for four days, it was decided that Suresh would take the first three days and seven and a half hours of the break, after which he also felt a sudden need to grab coffee and walked out of the room.

It became clear that Suresh really wasn't going anywhere during the holidays, and even if he were to go somewhere, he didn't seem to really care that the problems would be escalated to his manager.

At the end of the day, everybody knew that this was all a big charade anyway. Although being on-call was usually a pain in the ass, the holidays tended to be, ironically, some of the most desirable times to be on-call. No one really pushed any new code to production, so there were rarely any failures or new problems that arose. The past five breaks there had been no issues.

It did mean, however, that whoever was on-call would have to, during their time of being on-call, be able to pick up the phone at any time. Failure to do so would result in an angry Suresh, and eventually Adi if Suresh felt like upsetting his boss.

"Can you take up any time, Adi?" asked Nirmala, trying to get the house involved in the game.

Ah, you may have played that card a bit too soon, friend.

"No, I can't. You guys should take it up. It is good training for your work to understand the system. Besides, I'm very busy in the afternoon and free time. I really don't have much time. I have many hobbies and other things to do, and I've already done my part when I was a young engineer like you guys. So, unless absolutely necessary, no. I won't take any time," Adi answered.

The next Monday at 7:00 p.m.

Adi stood up from the couch in his home, carrying a big blue-and-white colored bowl filled with an Indian mixture. He looked around the room, chewing. His house was, for the most part, empty. Just a couple of pieces of furniture here and there adorned the place. A cloth couch and a set of a square table with one chair that were originally meant for outdoor sitting, but given their low price had ended up in Adi's living room.

Outside light shone in through the sliding doors that led to an empty space right outside his apartment. He walked over to his kitchen and put his decorated plate down on top of the counter and opened a cabinet to the lower-left of the stove, revealing its contents. Bags of Indian mixtures filled up all the space available. Adi took an open bag and poured himself a bowlful. He smiled as he sealed up the open bag with one of those metallic twirly things he got whenever he bought the white bread he loved at the store. He shut the cabinet door and walked back into the living room.

As he did so, he noticed that the sun was going down and soon there would be no more light in his apartment. So, he went over to the light controls and turned on the light of the ceiling fan and also lowered the level of the fan from a three to a one because three was only reserved for the daytime. All the while he struggled to not drop his giant, precious bowl of Indian mixture. Finally, he sat back down on his cloth couch, looked down at his bowl, and took a handful. The whirring of the ceiling fan wound down.

Back at the meeting room, 10:15 a.m.

"So, no one is going to volunteer? We only need eight more minutes covered, guys. John?" Adi asked with a small smile on his face, just enough to reveal his sparkling-white teeth.

"Adi, can you really not take up those eight minutes on Monday evening? Are you really going to be that busy during the break?" asked Nirmala in a brisk tone. Only she and John remained in the room.

Lately, the engineers had started to really scale-up the passive-aggressiveness. Every time someone escalated their tone, John imagined himself in a third-person point of view and thought that whoever was watching would certainly be having a good time.

"No, no. I'm very busy. I can't," said Adi. "What are you doing in that time, Nirmala?"

Oof.

The next Monday at 7:05 p.m., in Adi's living room

He liked to do this thing where he would try to fit as much mixture as possible in his mouth while still being able to crunch it up with his powerful molar at least once per mixture-eating session. That day was no different. Adi took handful after handful of mixture and stuffed his mouth with it.

Back in the meeting room, 10:40 a.m.

Nirmala gave a brief answer on how she would be busy remodeling her outdoor garden and that this was the only time she could do it because her gardener Francisco was booked up every other day of the week.

John knew for a fact that the more details people included in their conversation, the more likely they were to be lying. However, he seriously doubted that Adi was aware of this.

Dinh and Suresh had come back into the room and buried themselves in their laptops.

Ten minutes passed and not a single engineer had spoken. The game had come to a standstill. Those eight minutes left to cover were really no issue to anyone in the room, but at this point, taking them would be a sign of defeat. Those eight minutes meant much more to any of them than just the time they would have to spend with their phone on 'loud.'

Those minutes were freedom, independence, free will, and self-worth. Taking them up meant bowing down to their manager, to their handler, to their master. It meant that the pressures of capitalism and the consumerist machine that was America would once again be triumphant, even amongst some of the self-diagnosed smartest, freest, most independent, people in the world.

On top of it all, and in the front of their minds, was the idea that this was a tech company, not a bank. They would not let themselves be treated as bankers, analysts, or any other miserable worker in Wall Street or any of the famous financial districts in cities around the United States of America.

John was going to take a stand for himself and hoped that the team would follow. He did not want to bow down and lose his first ever on-call poker. He would not volunteer. Why did he have to?

He was the youngest and most inexperienced engineer in the team. If something did end up going terribly wrong during the on-call period, he would probably have to call someone else to assist him. It made sense to John that it was actually in everybody's, including the company they all worked for's, best interest for him not to be on-call during those eight minutes.

Nirmala excused herself to the restroom.

"Okay, guys, I don't have time for this. John, you take them up," exclaimed Adi, standing up.

"Sure," muttered John.

Well played.

The next Monday at 7:40 p.m., Adi's living room

"Man…that is some great fucking mixture!" proclaimed Adi to his non-existent audience. He had finished all the mixture in the bowl. Some days, if he was feeling feisty or in need of some extra serotonin, he would even go and get a second one of it. But today, the extra satisfaction would only be marginal.

He washed the dishes then went back to his living room. It was dark out now.

He took out a notebook with a pen stuffed in it from below the sofa he sat on and opened it.

The notebook, covered with his writing, was almost finished cover to cover. Adi scribbled away with a big smile on his face.

Back in the meeting room

"Okay," continued Adi. "Now that we have that figured out, shall we move on to planning? Or is it planning for planning?"

John never got to give his report, nor did he get any convincing answers from the people he had been emailing and messaging throughout the meeting. He certainly did not get an answer from his PM, but again, he didn't really care too much.

4.

A couple of weeks later, lunch time, in the company cafeteria

John sat down at the far end of the cafeteria, hoping that only Neveah would show up to their lunch meeting. She was one of the three people with whom John had made some semblance of a connection. Carson, a young engineer from San Antonio, Texas, and Luis Filipe, an ambitious and enthusiastic—a bit too much of that for John's taste—Brazilian financial analyst, were the two others.

There had been some sprinkled encounters here and there with the rest of the folks he had met in his first couple of weeks at the company. They were simply NPCs—non-playable characters, as John liked to call them. They gave him nothing new to think or worry about, and he did not give them anything back. He was an NPC to them.

These encounters would happen on runs for coffee in the middle of the afternoon, during his brief one-week stint at the gym, or even the walk to the office. But for the most part, every interaction John had with one of them went something along the lines of:

"John! Hey! Long time no see! Oh, gosh, it seems like it's been forever. Far too long! That much I know. Everything alright? How's work? Things?"

"Hey! [insert random person's name] long time no see indeed! Well, yeah everything is…fine? Things could definitely be better, but you know how it is. Actually..."

"Well, it was good catching up! Let's set something up?"

"Let's."

They never did. And that was okay by John.

Carson seemed like a good dude. He usually dressed in cargo shorts or pants and one of three types of shirts: a free company T-shirt, a free college hackathon T-shirt, which John was sure he had won many of, or a free tech conference T-shirt. His glasses were thin-rimmed and had a bridge above the nose that did not do his square face any favors.

However, he was a very nice guy and certainly book-smart. His team, the one in charge of developing a comprehensive artificial intelligence solution that would link together a bunch of areas of the company, was one of the most coveted and competitive teams. Only the brightest and hardest-working people worked there, usually with more education than just a Bachelor's degree. Carson had graduated college with a Master's degree in four years.

He was the type of kid who John would have tried to avoid socializing with outside of the Engineering quad. John thought he was cooler than the average student in the Engineering school, which was the pool of people Carson belonged to as far as John was concerned. Most of John's friends were not from the Engineering school, apart from a couple of people whose main group of friends were also not part of the Engineering school.

John was never rude to these nerds, as he would label them in his mind, and not only because those friendships came in useful when it was time to pick partners for a group project or to form a study group, but because he genuinely enjoyed their company. Just not outside the Engineering quad.

Carson was a strange mixture of awkward but confident. He was sure of who he was and did not back off from that fact. An awkward guy. Even though John was not, he respected the fact that Carson owned up to it.

Luis Filipe, on the other hand, was an energetic fella unlike anyone John had met before. People with whom he went to college and high school always seemed preoccupied with one thing or another, be it exams, job search, or relationships, to the point where it sometimes became crippling. Luis Filipe lived his life the way John wanted to live it: without restraints.

In the brief month since John had met him, Luis Filipe had already painted a full picture of what it was to grow up in a rich family in Brazil, going to casinos and getting drunk starting senior year of high school, although John had a strong suspicion that at least one of those two habits had started earlier than Luis chose to disclose. Luis Filipe was always very happy to see everybody he ran into, greeting John and strangers with a big smile on his face.

"Hello! *Tudo bem*?" he would say to strangers. "My name is Luis Filipe, and I'm from São Paulo. Where are you from, friend?"

Luis Filipe had come to do his undergraduate degree in the United States because he could afford it and was smart enough to get into a decent business school, per his parents' request. His mom was a high-ranking officer in one of Brazil's largest banks, and his dad was an executive-level director at a mining company. A true Brazilian power couple.

But John's favorite out of all of them was Neveah. Although he had not known her for very long, John had already developed a small crush on her. She worked in a mobile app development team John's team interacted with every once in a while.

Through these meetings and the times they'd gotten lunch together, John had learned how caring and relaxed she was. She conducted her life in admirable ways, always involved in political action and asking her friends how they were doing. John had been fortunate enough to have been asked that question a couple of times already. She was a breath of fresh air in a world where his air was seemingly polluted by a never-ending California fire season.

John had let Carson and his roommate know a couple of times already that he had a small crush on her, because God knows he could never shut his mouth about those things.

"Yeah, man, I don't know what it is, but she's just very smart and kind," John would say.

"Yeah, she's great, man, very cute and fun," Carson would usually reply.

It didn't take many more interactions like these for John to believe beyond a shadow of a doubt that his good friend Carson also had developed a bit of a crush on Neveah.

That day, Carson was the first one of the pack to grab his food and find John in the corner of the cafeteria. Usually people waved at each other emphatically in the cafeteria but John was always embarrassed to do so. He would pretend not to see his friends until they were literally inches from him.

"Oh, hey, Carson, I didn't see you coming."

"Yeah, John, for some reason you're always looking in every direction except the one I'm coming from. I guess you're just bad at it." Carson sat opposite John at the table. "Didn't know someone could be bad at that."

"I guess I am bad at it," admitted John, relieved he was out of that little hole. "What you got there, some salad from the bar? The salad bar?"

"Yeah, it kind of gets the job done. I've been trying to be a little healthier and lose some weight. These cheap leaves are helping me get there. Although I must admit, they're not even that cheap."

John looked down at his plate and admired his self-collapsing cheeseburger and onion rings so fried they could be coal rings.

I guess I could get a salad next time.

"You do know, Carson, that salads are not really that much healthier than regular food? That's just a myth that the big salad corporations have been trying to push on the public. People have lived for thousands of years just fine without salads. How come they weren't essential until recently?"

"Are you being serious or trying to be funny? I don't think anything you just said is accurate, John." Carson took a big bite of the crunchy leaves. Then, as he chewed, he said, "Do you actually believe that?"

John didn't believe a word he had said, but he couldn't let Carson win the argument.

Why did I say that stupid shit about fucking salads? Lived for thousands of years? Come on, John.

"Yeah, I believe it. To a degree."

"Whatever, man, can we talk about something else?"

"Mmm hmmm," he managed and nodded with his mouth filled with cheeseburger.

"Okay, I just wanted to tell you something before Neveah gets here."

John forgot to finish chewing and swallowed.

I fucking knew it. Bastard.

"Sure, what's up?"

"I think I…Neveah is really cute, right? I think I'm developing a bit of a crush on her," Carson said.

The shadow of a doubt had been confirmed.

"Yeah, man, I agree. I guess it's fine if both of us like her. I don't think she would fall for either of us," said John, looking him straight in the eye.

"For sure, she probably has a boyfriend, or something or other. Everybody in the Bay Area is either taken or at least pretending to be. Well, let's both agree to back off then, I guess, and if she falls for either one of us then so be it."

"I'm okay with that."

John was very okay with that. He didn't really see Carson as a rival in the game of dating and love. John was certain that at the end of the day, he would be the one to end up with Neveah. There was nothing more certain in his life.

Kid doesn't stand a chance.

They both decided that waiting for someone else to eat at the work cafeteria was not a necessity. Everybody had busy schedules, and they would show up when they could. After a couple of minutes of silence and food consumption, Neveah and Luis Filipe showed up at the same time, each with the cafeteria's special of the day: Fried Pork Noodles or, as John liked to call it, "The completely normal and average fried pork noodles."

"Hey, guys," said John. "Glad you could make it. Are those… fried pork noodles?"

"Hey, John. Hi, Carson! Yeah, they're the fried pork noodles special. They're alright, sustenance," said Neveah.

"Hello, my friends! How are you? And you? I'm doing great, never been better," said Luis Filipe enthusiastically.

"I haven't checked the markets yet today. I take it crypto is doing well today?" said Carson.

"Oh, my friend, it is wonderful. It is up forty percent, just today! And it is still going up. This is crazy," replied Luis Filipe. "At this rate, I will have double the money by the end of the week."

"Yeah, that shit's nuts," John intervened. "I knew this kid in college who had invested in crypto way back when, maybe like, fifty dollars' worth? I can't even imagine how much he's got nowadays."

"Well, I don't think it's a very safe market," said Neveah, visibly worried. "I mean, just last month the thing was worth less than a dollar and now it's at over two thousand? It's bound to come back down. Don't be stupid, guys. I don't want to see anybody lose all their quote unquote hard-earned money. Just do what I do and invest in index funds."

"Index funds, schmindex funds!" said Luis Filipe, smiling. Then he banged the table with the back of his fork. "Crypto is where it's at, baby! Before you know it, I'll be out of this fucking place and back to São Paulo, riding around in my red Ferrari like a deus. You guys are, of course, welcomed to visit any time. Any time."

Then he scarfed down a big chunk of noodles and pork with a fork and spoon.

"I hope it works out, man," said Carson. "Just be careful. You never know what's gonna happen."

"Don't...worry about it...big man," said Luis Filipe through his food, some of it diving back onto his plate.

Neveah turned to Carson. "Well, I'm just happy we can all meet. I know it's been a while. Thank you, Carson, for sending out those calendar invites. Otherwise, I don't think we could have been able to figure this out! You're the real MVP of the day."

"I know, in this day and age, it's so much easier to get everybody on the same page that way," said Carson.

John hated the idea of having to RSVP to a lunch meeting with his friends on an email service. He was more old school than that. If relationships and friendships were meant to happen, then they would happen organically, and not through an email list.

"Yeah, Carson. Thanks for sending the invites," he said.

"So, John, how are you doing?" asked Neveah, turning to him. "Last time we spoke, I remember you said you weren't doing so great. Having a tough time settling into the job?"

"Well, I'm…I'm doing alright, you know? Work is driving me crazy. And it hasn't even been that long! My boss doesn't seem like he knows what he's doing half the time, and I keep getting pulled in all sorts of directions. I feel like I never get anything done."

He leaned back on his chair and ran his fingers through his hair, stretching it out to a point of slight pain. "Now that I say that out loud, yeah, I don't think I'm doing so hot, guys."

"Yikes, sorry to hear that," she said. "I know this is a bit private, but did you end up going to see a therapist? I remember you talking about it last time. My therapist has really helped me work some stuff out. I still talk to the one I have from college."

"Yeah, man, therapy is great. I went all through college," said Carson.

Did you really? Or are you just saying that?

John could hear the chomping of Carson's iceberg lettuce as if he were taking the bites directly in his eardrum. "Yeah, I actually did but she didn't really help me very much. I think therapy just isn't for me. She was not very understanding of where I was coming from. I came out of that session a hundred dollars poorer and just as fucked up."

A week ago, at Dr. Jane's office

Dr. Jane Ellway is considered a true pioneer and the definition of success amongst her colleagues. She had written a couple of books that dealt precisely with the sorts of feelings and stresses that John was experiencing.

John sat on a chair in front of her. She had her legs crossed and a big yellow notepad on her lap, a very traditional therapist look.

"Doctor…"

"Yes, John?"

"Do you know what fear of roaming black holes is?"

"I don't think I do. What's that?"

John rested his chin on his palms, which made it difficult to talk clearly. "Well, it's this thing where you are constantly in fear that a black hole could come close enough to the Earth to swallow it whole. If that happens, then there's really nothing you can do except fall into this dark gravitational pit and slowly become spaghettified, at least according to some people."

"That is very interesting. I did not know that. Thank you for sharing."

John raised his head. "No, I don't think you get it, Doctor. Just imagine for a second. Humor me on this one, will you?"

"Okay, John. What should I—"

"You are going about your day, walking your dog, your cat, whatever it is people your age do in the afternoons. And all of a sudden, the sky goes dark. No one knows what's happening. You look up, and you just see things flying off the surface of the Earth into space. And again, I cannot stress this enough, there is *nothing* you can do about it except fly away with the rest of them. And it could happen at any time. Could happen now, could happen five minutes from now. No one knows. That's the beauty of it."

"Well, John, does that make you anxious, thinking about these roaming black holes?"

"Not really. I just find it fascinating that some people do."

Back at the cafeteria

"Maybe you could try a new therapist? Sometimes you have to go through a couple to find the one who fits you," said Neveah in a stern but sweet voice.

"Yeah, I don't think so. I think these are things that I need to work out on my own. I don't think anyone could help me. All they do is sit there and ask you how you're feeling until the hour runs out and they can cash their check."

"Damn," said Carson. "You must have had a really bad therapist. I'm sorry, man."

At Dr. Jane's office, five minutes after the last time

"All I want to know, Doctor, is why they stopped after *The Godfather Part III*. I know Michael Corleone is dead, yadda yadda. But his daughter is still alive, right? She could become the new mafia boss girl and lay down the law. I would watch three more movies of that shit. Hell, even ten more! Francis Ford Coppola is a quitter."

Back at the cafeteria

"My friend," said Luis Filipe, "if it is any consolation, in Brazil, there is no such thing as therapy. It is just you and yourself."

"Luis," said Carson, "don't be stupid. I'm pretty sure therapy exists in Brazil."

"Maybe those pussies over in Rio have therapy but not in São Paulo. In São Paulo, we party! And learn finance in the United States, of course. Like yours truly."

"Luis Filipe!" said Neveah. "How many times do I need to tell you we don't say that word here!"

"I apologize, my lady. You know I mean no harm."

John and Carson both shot glares at Luis Filipe.

Wait. Does this motherfucker like her too?

At Dr. Jane's office, five minutes after last time

"So, Doctor, let me get this straight. You're telling me that the whole world is out to get me? That I need to be careful and really only care for myself? That even though my manager is probably right, I should not listen to him and just do whatever I feel is right?

Dr. Ellway sat forward in her chair, pulled her hair back, and looked up at John with a stern face. "John, that is literally the opposite of what I just said."

Back at the cafeteria

"I think I'm just gonna stick to my walks and go from there," said John.

"Whatever floats your metaphorical boat, friend," said Carson.

The rest of the meal went pretty much how John thought it would. Everybody complained about a couple of things, mostly what they had already complained about in the past.

As they all stood up to leave, Neveah and Luis Filipe made their way first to put away their dirty dishes.

John pulled Carson aside. "Remember our deal."

"Yeah, I remember, man. You don't have to worry about me."

I know I don't. He probably thinks he has a chance. He is wearing better shoes than I am. Should I get some?

Exactly ten years later, inside a big house in Redwood City

"So, dear, I've been thinking of what we should name our new son. Do you like Jack? Like the Ripper but not really. I would want it to mean something else."

"Carson, you know I don't have time for this," said Neveah as she bent over to pick up some toy cars.

"Yeah, I guess you're right. We still have time."

"Well, we do know one thing for sure."

"What's that?"

"We're not going to call him John!"

They both had a good laugh about that one for a while.

5.

That same day, 5:30 p.m., at the company

Please pick up. Please pick up.

John tightly held his phone up to his ear with the palm of his hand. He had learned to hold it that way as opposed to the natural way of holding it by its side with fingers because his phone had the audacity and tendency to unlock and dial numbers mid-call at will. Every time that would happen, John would experience a mini-rage moment.

It was little bugs and problems with technology that would get to him the most. His room's door could be jammed and not open properly for weeks, but God forbid his phone auto-corrected the word *fuck* to *duck*.

He occupied his other hand with the task of holding back his hair from his forehead as he rocked back and forth in his seat, limited in his movement.

Please, for the love of God, Suresh, pick up your damn phone.

He shook one leg as a way to relieve some anxiety, as he kept the other one firmly grounded. He felt like a complete circuit, with ground and power outlets working in harmony, better than any he had ever built in his one electrical engineering class.

No answer from Suresh. He took the phone away from his head and stared at the screen, looking for another contact.

The phone's brightness illuminated John's face inside the dark bathroom stall. The small light above his head had gone out, so only the illumination that seeped in through the cracks at the top, bottom, and next to the door of the stall complemented his phone's. He had a small, but sure, look at the bathroom door from his position.

John sat on the toilet, pants down to only one of his ankles, and shirt tied to his stomach. It was hot inside the men's first-floor bathroom of the company, hotter than it had ever been. The heat, combined with the day's worth of excrement and piss made for an abhorrent atmosphere that surrounded John inside his cell composed of four plastic walls.

The hinges of the door opening loudly caught John's attention. He peeped through the hole in the stall's door. A small Hispanic woman walked inside.

"Excuse me! Excuse me! I am going to clean the bathroom, okay? Take your time! I will be outside. No worries!"

She then proceeded to put the *Out of Service* sign on the door, leaving it open yet blocked. John felt exposed with his pants down and almost out, although he was certain that no one could really see him, even if they looked closely as they walked in front of the bathroom door.

Okay, at least no one else is going to come in here.

He went back to his phone and looked for a different contact he could call.

God fucking damn it. I fucking hate scooters. Who came up with the idea? And why? Why?

He dialed Luis Filipe's number. He figured that, even though he didn't know him that well, Luis Filipe was a man who would sympathize with the perilous situation he found himself in. To John's dismay, however, the call went straight to voicemail.

"Hello, friend. You have tried to reach me and I did not pick up the phone. Don't worry, I will call you back eventually. Have a nice day!"

John's options were running out and some executive decisions would have to be taken, and taken soon. The entrance of the Hispanic lady indicated that his time in the stall was not boundless.

1:46 p.m., three hours and forty-four minutes earlier

"Hi, two large coffees, please!" said John, looking closely at the employee's name tag. "Ms. Gonzalez, is it?"

John and Suresh stood at the cafeteria's shop in line for their usual after-lunch coffee. The one-hour lunch time he took and coffee time right after lunch were two separate occasions that deserved their own dedicated time.

"Yes, nice pronunciation!" replied Ms. Gonzalez. "How do you guys like your coffees?"

My seven years of Spanish are finally being put to good use.

"I'll take mine with a bit of sugar, please," jumped in Suresh.

John continued, "I'll take mine black, as is. Thanks."

"Sure thing, I'll get you guys those coffees right away," said Ms. Gonzalez, writing down names and preparations on their respective cups.

Suresh grabbed John's arm. "Large cups? I did not consent to such proportions."

"You don't have to finish it," said John. "The extra cost between the medium and the large is only seventy-five cents. It just makes sense to get the large even if you don't finish it."

John really admired the art of coffee making, even though in this particular case there wasn't much of an art to it. Still, the way she prepared them relaxed him. He thought of himself as a connoisseur. He even had a French press at home and had only replaced the glass bottle two times, to his own and his roommate's surprise.

"Besides," he continued, "I might just finish yours if you don't."

"That's kind of gross, isn't it?" said Suresh.

"Very much so, yeah. I don't know what the fuck I was thinking. I just need this right now, you know? Sometimes you just need that coffee to fuck you up, to make you feel like you can rule the world."

"John," said Suresh. "Please tell me you've never done coke?"

"No, I haven't."

"Don't."

Back in the men's first-floor bathroom, ten minutes later

John very carefully removed his pants from the remaining leg. He took the boxers out of the pants and laid the two side by side, examining them.

To his disillusionment, there were dark brown stains on both his underwear and outerwear, even their outer parts. And they smelled like shit, because that's what was on them. His own shit.

God fucking damn it, John. How do we get ourselves in these situations?

Whenever John did something tense or time-sensitive, his mind immediately went to the wonderful tune of *In the Hall of the Mountain King*. This tune had reverberated in his head during the first time he took the SAT, the second time he took the SAT, and every time he removed a tonsil stone.

He took a piece of toilet paper and rolled it up neatly, making sure that the point of contact was small, yet firm. And then the tune started playing.

Using one hand, he picked up the underwear and placed it closer to the toilet, which really was just a couple of inches of movement but valuable inches. And then he went to work, trying desperately to get as much of the stain out as possible. He needed this to work.

3:30 p.m. the same day

John walked into the break room to find a snack. It was that time of day to scourge the area for any leftover fruit or granola bars.

A suspiciously fresh-looking pear sat alone in the transparent-doored fridge. Usually, by that time, all the good fruit would be gone. John much preferred apples, bananas, oranges, really any food, over pears, but leaving a pear of this quality behind at that hour would have been a capital sin.

John walked over, opened the fridge, and picked it up for examination. There was nothing wrong with it, at least that he could tell using his limited expertise in fruit.

On his way out of the break room, with his beautiful pear, he walked past the instant coffee machine.

He looked at a wall-clock, then back at the machine.

Okay, fine. If you insist.

Back in the bathroom, five minutes later

Okay, John, what have you done?

The mess on his clothes had almost doubled in area. He had made the rookie mistake of not patting but trying to rub the stains out. He had made plenty of mistakes that day, but this one somehow made its way to the top of John's rankings of them.

In the Hall of the Mountain King had been replaced by his mother's nagging.

"John!" she would say, after trying to clean up splashed ketchup in the dining room tablecloth. "How many times do I have to tell you to *not* spread the ketchup but to dab it up instead! Dab it up, John, dab it up!"

Dab it up. To be fair, Mother never prepared me for this.

It was too late, the damage was done, and he was stuck in the stall with practically unwearable clothes. For a second, he considered the idea of just ignoring all social norms and rules and going home with stained pants. But the thought quickly faded; the train ride was at least an hour home, and it wouldn't be fair to the other passengers. Not that anything that had happened to him that day was precisely fair, but that was not the other passengers' faults. At least not all of them.

The Hispanic woman came back in, ducking under the sign that hung over the door. "Hello, sir? Sir? Are you still in there?"

"Yes, sorry, I'll be out soon. I'm so sorry."

A different Hispanic lady came around to check in on her coworker. "*¿Qué está pasando? ¿Por qué no sale el muchacho del baño?*"

"*Ay amiga, pues creo que aquí el joven se cagó los pantalones.*"

The other Hispanic woman gasped and put her hand over her mouth. "*No me digas. ¿Se cagó?*"

"*Se cagó.*"

"*Jesús, María y José. ¿Lo viste cagarse? ¿Por qué se cagó?*"

"*¿Cómo chingados voy a saber por qué el joven aquí se cagó? No sé amiga, namás lo encontré ahí metido,*" she said while pointing at the stall.

Then, the two of them left the bathroom and were out of John's hearing range.

John had understood enough from what the two women had said to know that they were aware of the unfortunate fact that he had pooped his pants.

Sí, me cagué.

4:55 p.m., at John's desk

John stood up, packed his things up, and picked up a large cup of coffee, downing whatever was left of it. He even swooshed the room temperature coffee in his mouth, through his teeth, before swallowing.

He threw it in the trash, next to two other large disposable cups. All three large disposable cups he had used in the past five hours rested all on top of each other with no spillage piled up at the bottom. They were all completely empty.

He normally would not have had this much coffee in a day, let alone an afternoon, but he figured that his lack of motivation and energy had to be due to his lack of caffeine and nothing else. He tried to get himself back into the mental state of constant impending doom he would find himself in college. This, mostly caused by his anxiety, in itself triggered by the ever-present fear of failing classes, but heavily aided by his consistent consumption of coffee and other caffeinated drinks.

It had to be that—a lack of caffeine. He had a good-paying job, and he hadn't even been in it long enough to become jaded, like other older coworkers he had met.

I feel fucking fantastic.

John headed down the five flights of stairs and out of the company.

He strutted confidently down the street, holding both of his backpack strands with one hand over his chest. The temperature was just right, too. It was that lovely perfect temperature he had always dreamed California would have.

Then, very, very faintly, John's stomach rumbled.

Back in the men's bathroom

His options were running out. He wasn't back in school where he could dial a hundred different numbers and ask for roadside assistance.

He could call Carson. But he didn't really want to.

Carson, although a good friend, was a greater enemy. Calling him would mean two things: not only did he, John, shit his pants, but that he had no other friend or person to call other than him. It would give Carson too much power.

What if he said he would come give him a new pair of pants but never showed up? What if he texted Neveah about it?

God forbid.

If he were to call Carson and ask for help, this would forever alter the scales of balance in the relationship. He who brings the pants to the shitted shall have the upper hand.

He for sure would tell Neveah.

John opened Carson's contact in his phone and looked around the stall. The situation was grim. The only clean clothes he had were his socks and shirt. It was not going to work out.

I guess I'll just have to kill him after he brings me the change of clothes. Yeah, that'll do.

So, he dialed Carson's number.

To his relief, Carson did not answer. But also to his complete feeling of despair, he did not answer, because he knew that Carson not answering his phone meant that there was only one other person he could call before he would have to literally start yelling for help, and who knows if anyone would even listen to the twenty-three year old madman in a toilet stall with shit in his pants. He knew he wouldn't.

Neveah would answer if I called her.

Back on the street, John walking home

I can make it to the train station. I can make it to the train station.

John wasn't sure he could make it to the train station. What had started as a faint rumbling had quickly evolved into a heavy churning of the guts. His stomach, unlike him, had not had a good day. John had not been kind to it, and it was letting him know.

He picked up the pace and tightened his legs closer together. This was not the first time John had been in this type of situation, and certainly wouldn't be the last one, but he had never, not once, not made it. Not even in the dark winter blizzards of the Midwest had John ever taken so much as a piss outside of a proper facility.

Only a couple of blocks away.

Then, coming from the train station, a man on a scooter looking at his phone scooted right in his direction. John had learned on his first day of work to avoid the scooters by stepping aside and letting them through. With resentment in his step, he did so. "You're not supposed to be on the sidewalk, you asshole bas—"

"Watch out!"

A completely different scooter, with a completely different person, going the direction of the train station, hit John dead-on.

For a moment, John was still in mid-air. He could feel the ground coming up to meet him just as much as he could feel the entire universe and skies above him.

He knew what would happen the moment he hit the ground. The perfect streak would be over. His system would win.

Not like this. Not. Like. This.

Eventually, he hit the ground. He did not move. He did not scream. He did not care for the fact that both his elbows were scraped. He did, regrettably, let go.

Back in the men's bathroom

John thought back to the dozens of movies that showcased people getting into ventilation ducts above rooms to get around buildings sneakily. How were those people not afraid to be stuck in such a place without any movement? What if they had to use the restroom? He despised the scenes.

He was trapped and his only escape would put him in another prison, a prison of loneliness. Or at least so he thought.

He opened his phone for the last time, and tapped on Neveah's contact, a tear slowly streaking down his cheek.

There is no other option.

He pressed on her number, just as a pair of fresh-looking pants slid under the stall door and hit his legs.

Through the crack, he saw the Hispanic woman smiling.

"Sir, here are some clean pants, okay? It happens to all of us. Just please leave the bathroom. I want to clean and go home."

"Thank you, so much, goodness. You are a literal lifesaver," said John, wiping off the tears from his face. "*Muchas gracias.*"

"*De nada.* But please, do hurry up."

John put his phone away and the pants on. They did not quite fit him like his own, but that was to be expected. He just tightened the belt a couple of holes more.

He threw away his pants and underwear in the trash cart brought to the bathroom by the Hispanic woman.

"Thank you so much, again. I'm sorry I took so long."

And so, John went on his way to the train station to catch a train not as fast as the bullet but not as slow as the local one.

Right as he got there, he saw a bunch of scooters, all lined up perfectly next to each other, like a small army of ducklings.

He picked up and threw four different scooters five to ten feet, and then also put the remaining ones on their sides as they all programmatically cried to be put upright. He did so with a psychopathic calmness.

Fuck these motherfucking scooters in this motherfucking town.

6.

____

A month later, 11:00 p.m., somewhere in Outer Richmond, San Francisco, CA

John stepped up to a staircase right on the edge of the sidewalk and stopped before continuing. Over the staircase stood a vine-infested arch at least a couple of decades old, parts of the paint, and even the concrete itself, cracking away. The arch had barely-visible writing engraved on it that read *Welcome Home.*

He took a deep breath in and out. If he had learned anything from his brief time with his therapist, it was how to take long, deep breaths in and out.

Is there even another way to breathe?

Even though therapy had not ended with him knowing how to fix his perspective on the world, he at least knew how to breathe now.

He took out his phone and checked the time. He had a couple of unopened texts from Carson and even a missed call from Neveah. It was also later than he thought. Much later.

He grudgingly hiked up the longer-than-expected flight of stairs toward the blatantly obnoxious noise coming from the second floor of the house.

9:30 p.m. (an hour and a half earlier) at John's apartment

John sat on his couch, dressed up, ready to go out, water still dripping from the back of his damp hair. He wore his classic jeans and a T-shirt with a clever design, this time paired with a green bomber jacket. That night he was trying out a new pair of sneakers, for which he felt a reserved amount of excitement.

New clothes or shoes were not really his thing. He usually wore the same pair of comfortable shoes for a whole year, sometimes more, depending on how long it would take his mother to think that it was time for her dear son Johnny to get new ones.

Tonight, however, he had planned his outfit in advance all of three hours before getting dressed. Neveah was going to be at the party and by God, would she see his new sneakers.

The question before going out every night was whether to take a shared ride to the night's destination. It would save John some money, a couple of dollars each time but would usually get him to his destination a bit later. Since the night before he had already traveled in a private ride, he was leaning more toward a shared one.

The couple of dollars add up.

Going on public transportation was by far the cheapest option, just over two dollars. The night's party, however, was happening across town all the way in Outer Richmond, nowhere near a convenient bus or MUNI route.

That was a big problem with San Francisco. John had expected better public transportation from a big city. Even though he took a decent amount of shared rides, he still considered himself to be a transit-oriented teen.

He pondered this conundrum as his hair dripped the last remnants of shower water on his hands.

Fuck it, it's early, I should save up, I'm taking this shared ride. I'm sure plenty of people are going that way anyway.

He selected "shared ride" on the app and a couple of minutes later, he got a notification on phone.

-Good news! We found a driver nearby. Carlos is on his way! Please be ready to be picked up.

Back at the house in Outer Richmond

John got to the top of the stairs and pushed open the already-slightly-open door.

What in the fuck is that smell? Goodness me.

The place had a stench comprised of a combination of moldy old-house walls and sweaty socks and shoes, with a hint of yellow-foot sprinkled on top. His sense of smell had taken him back to his dorm's small gym locker room, that is if the locker room were also in a house ready to fall apart from the parasitic infestation of mold and God knows what other microorganisms. Needless to say, John gagged a bit.

A sign hung next to the entrance which read *Please take your shoes off or vacuum my carpet. Thank you!*

Well, that makes sense.

He closed the door behind him and started to walk into the apartment before running into dozens of shoes on the floor, blocking the path. John kicked some aside around him, making enough space to go down on one knee and untie his shoes, his new precious sneakers. He picked them up and placed them in a spot where he would be able to find them easily on the way out.

After placing his shoes, John was met by a stranger, or at least someone who seemed to be a stranger. It could have very easily been someone he had already met but forgotten.

"Hey, there, welcome to the party!"

"Hey, thanks," said John. "Sorry I'm late." He felt he needed to apologize to this girl, who appeared to be the host, or at least playing the part.

"Oh, don't worry about it! We're just getting started," she replied.

John felt somewhat relieved.

"So," she continued. "May I offer you a drink? We have some wine and some local craft beer. If you want to smoke, there's a crowd of people out in the back, on the balcony. And no, in case you were going to ask, we do not have a hallucinogens room. That was the last party, and things got out of hand."

"Oh, man…umm…I'll just take whatever people are not taking. I hate when things are left behind at my apartment, so I'll try and do my part."

"The Milk Stout it is then. Some guy brought it at the beginning of the party and it has been just sitting there. Thanks for volunteering."

What the fuck is a milk stout?

"Oh, perfect, I love Milk Stouts."

"Okay, cool, I'll be right back!"

Unsure of whether to follow the aforementioned girl, John stood in place and took out his phone to text the group chat he had with Neveah, Carson, and Luis Filipe.

"John, man!" said Carson, who came into John's view with Neveah at his side, parting the sea of people in between them. "Where have you been? We've been waiting for you a while."

"Yeah," added Neveah. "Is everything alright? We already sang happy birthday."

"Yeah, yeah, everything's fine," answered John. "You guys know how it is sometimes with the shared rides. Sometimes you win the lottery and go straight to wherever the fuck you're going, and sometimes you just get unequivocally fucked. Sometimes you ride the van, and sometimes the van rides you. Today, folks, I was the ridee."

He paused for a split second.

"Happy Birthday?" he continued. "I thought this was a going away party. Isn't Sam or something moving back to New York? Is it also her birthday?" He paused again. "Also, it's not even midnight."

"Sam's thing is next weekend," said Neveah. "This is Jenny's birthday. Her birthday is today, John, not tomorrow, so we sang happy birthday for her, you know, like friends and normal people do."

John and company were all of a sudden distracted by two people who ran into the party, coming in from the outside balcony, yelling, giggling, and poking each other with silver wands with stars attached at the end of them. One of them had fishnets on with strong eyeliner, while the other one had an orange onesie and plastic crocs-like shoes on. They blazed through the crowd and vanished upstairs to the third floor as quickly as they had come into the room.

"What in the world was that?" asked John

"In a world…" said Carson, trying to make his best impression of Sir David Attenborough. "Where San Francisco males have to get the attention of the limited San Francisco females, the mating rituals become rather…absurd. But in a society such as this one, there is no other option left for the poor San Francisco males but to put on, say, a fantastic show and play along with any games that might have been put on the table."

"I'm pretty sure that's just drugs," said Neveah.

John remained perplexed.

"I would concur," said Carson.

Would you also concur that you're a giant bitch?

Neveah and Carson led John through the party straight into the kitchen, in hopes of finding the host who had promised to give John a Milk Stout Beer. Instead, they ran into someone they had met at the party previously that night.

"Hey, Michelangelo!" said Carson. "This is my friend John. I think the two of you should meet."

John and Michelangelo exchanged pleasantries.

Carson turned to John and said, "I think you'd be quite interested in what Michelangelo has been working on. He actually started his own company while at school and moved out here before finishing up his senior year, or at least that's what he told me."

Michelangelo chuckled. "Something like that, yeah."

"Well," Carson continued. "We'll leave you two to it. Neveah and I are gonna walk around, see who else is here, say hello, all the things."

Ah, here it is. The fabled Silicon Valley Startup of golden promises and infinite riches.

It had taken a while, but John was finally encountering one out in the wild. He had even started to believe that they were not real, that these young Silicon Valley startup jerks were made up and romanticized by the media. But this man here, this man…he had it all. The name, which couldn't possibly be his real name, the look, the attitude, the feel. John was eager to hear all about the Series C funding, about the expansion plans and options distribution.

I want to hear all about it. Lay it on me, brother.

9:35 p.m., outside of John's apartment

John stepped up to a black Honda Odyssey on the sidewalk next to his apartment. The door opened without him having to touch it, and he hopped in. John quickly noticed the darker complexion of the man behind the wheel, as well as a strong Hispanic accent, so he made sure to put his seven years of middle school and high school Spanish to use. He rolled the "r" in the middle of his name.

"Hey, for John? Carlos?" said John as he strapped in his seatbelt.

"Yes, John. I am Carlos."

Carlos did not turn his body greet him, but through the small glimpse in the rearview mirror, John discerned traces of a tired, puffed-up face, plagued with remnants of old acne scars that never really went away.

John always tried to make the determination the moment he stepped up in a shared ride of whether the driver was someone who wanted to talk to him, someone who was worth talking to, or someone he simply should not say a word to. With Carlos, he was conflicted.

"So, how's your night going?" asked John. "Busy? Fridays I imagine are busy."

"Fridays are…busy, yes. Sometimes Thursdays are more busier than Fridays, but yesterday was not too busy, so today Friday is busy. Yes."

"Gotcha, gotcha…"

Ooh, I think I just opened el "caja de pandorro!"

"Eh, so where are you going? Outer Richmond, is that right?" asked Carlos.

"Yeah, I think so? I've never really been over there," replied John cautiously.

"You think so? Let's check again. I got it right here, don't worry, boss. Yeah, you are going all the way out there. We might pick up a couple of people on the way."

"Yeah, probably."

"So, where are you from? You don't look like you're from here. You tech? You look like you work in tech or something like that. Tell me I'm wrong."

"You're not. I do in fact do tech. I work in San Jose. I actually just moved here a couple of months ago to start the job, but I'm originally from the Midwest."

"I don't get it."

"Get what?"

"The Midwest."

"What's not to get?"

"It's not really west, and it's also not really middle of the country. It is more like middle north. That would make more sense. Midnorth."

John briefly questioned his existence. "I guess so. But actually, the name is more of a historical name. See…"

"We're not in history, so they should change the name. It is confusing for people like me, who did not grow up here."

"Where are you from?"

"I was born in Guatemala City, have you heard of it?"

"Is that the capital of Guatemala?"

Carlos smiled. "Yes, it is the capital of Guatemala. Shit place, not good anymore. But it is where I was born. I came here only in the seventies and have lived all over the place. But I settled here in California, and then San Francisco because of the wife. She was from here so I followed her."

"Yeah? How's she doing?"

Back at the party

"So then," continued Michelangelo. "People can update their progress daily right here and bam! More connections."

"Okay, okay…tell me more," said John, standing close to Michelangelo, arms crossed.

Back at the shared ride

"And then one day," said Carlos. "I found out she was the biggest whore that America had ever seen. I walk in to our little house after a long day of work. And what do I find, if not dinner and a welcome kiss? I find her on the couch with another man's cock in her mouth. In my own house. Can you believe that? Not even a big penis, small penis. Small man too. Small white man. I think he was bald. Not strong hair like mine."

At this point, Carlos looked back and made a sign with his fingers separated only by a couple of inches. "Small, small penis."

"Oh, man," said John. "That's awful. I'm sorry to hear that."

"I walked out and have only seen the bitch a couple of times since. I'm very close with my daughter, who lives with me. My angel, Maria. But now I think she's dating some white man so it's not the best. No offense, buddy."

"Yeah, none taken, we do some pretty fucked-up stuff every once in a while like putting our dicks in other men's wives' mouths."

Too far?

Back at the party

"Carson!" John frantically screamed, trying to locate his friend. "Carson! Have you seen Carson?" asked John to an unimportant partygoer. "I need to tell him something right now!"

He dragged Michelangelo with him through the party until they found Carson and Neveah talking in a corner.

"Carson! There you are!"

"What is it, John? Are you okay?"

John caught his breath and gathered himself. "Carson, have you heard this shit?"

"What? What shit?" Carson replied.

"Michelangelo's app! It's fucking brilliant."

Carson let out a controlled laugh and raised his eyebrows at Neveah before turning back to John.

"Yeah, I have. I hear he's doing quite well for himself." Carson nodded to Michelangelo who responded with a nod of his own.

"I mean," continued John. "I don't know why no one had thought about it before."

"Yeah, I don't know," replied Carson. "Once you think about it a bit, it actually makes a lot of sense."

"Yeah, yeah, it does!" said John.

Luis Filipe came in from behind, high-fiving everyone in his way and kissing the girls and guys on the cheeks as his way of greeting.

"Luis Filipe! The man of the hour!" said John.

"My friends, Neveah, Carson, John," said Luis Filipe. "I am the man of the year! The way this crypto be risin', we might never see tomorrow!"

"That sounds like a bad thing," said Neveah.

"Exactly," said Luis Filipe, puzzling her. "So what's going on here? Is this party poppin' or what?"

Luis Filipe had shaved everything but his mustache and wore jeans and a black leather jacket, a very eighties look, which made John's outfit seem simple and unimpressive.

"Luis Filipe!" said John. "You gotta hear this shit, man. My guy here Michelangelo has an app that he's working on."

"Working on is an understatement," said Michelangelo. "We just secured Series C funding."

Almost Bingo!

"Series C!" John slapped Michelangelo on the back. "That's insane, man."

"Well, what is it?" asked Luis Filipe. "What is my fat Brazilian ass going to invest money into?"

"It's a new social network..." said John, building the anticipation. "For balding men! They can do all sorts of shit, like share their balding progress, support each other, share techniques for slowing it down, some balding hairstyles. Whatever the case may be! It's called...Bald Brotherhood."

Luis Filipe stared at Michelangelo quietly, now in charge of the anticipation in the group.

"What do you think?" asked John.

Back at the shared ride

"A little too far, little man. A little too far," said Carlos.

"Sorry, yeah, sorry. I do that sometimes," said John.

John was never sure what to say to people who shared more than they should have. Was he supposed to be engaging or just understanding? He didn't want to act like a therapist, no way, but he didn't want to act like a dick.

This time, he had missed the mark, but it had been a hard mark to hit. Carlos's marital problems had climbed up the ladder of John's "bizarre stories" leaderboard, passing his freshman year's roommate story about dung beetles and their effects on his bonsai at home, and his uncle Jim's story about the time he swears he met Jennifer Aniston at the local Meijer and almost fell in love.

"We are stopping now to pick up a young lady."

The van pulled over next to a yoga studio, and a young woman in yoga attire, which included a yoga mat on her back, hopped into the van. She visibly wore wireless in-ear headphones.

"Hey, for Kim?"

"Yes, Kim." replied Carlos.

"Thanks."

John sat up straight in his seat and widened his leg stance. The door started to close, but the van started moving quickly before it shut completely. Not a couple of seconds later, Carlos's phone rang again to signal him that a new passenger had been added to the ride. John could never help himself, whenever he was in a shared ride, but to look at the phone of the driver and assess their approach toward their new customer.

He called it backseat ride-sharing. He would pay close attention to the driver's phone and constantly check how far they were from picking up their new rider. Drivers usually had the navigation system on their phone screen, which John then used to check their route. Every time a driver missed a turn or looked as if they deliberately chose a different route, John would wince. He couldn't help but look every single time. He knew he could not intervene or do anything about it, but, contrary to his self-described stoicism, he would care. A lot.

Similarly, whenever John ordered food online, he would keep the phone application open and track his driver's movements through the city. This parted from the fact that whenever he ordered food, it came as a last-second decision, by which time John was already awfully hungry. He called that home-seat delivering.

The approach to this next pick-up seemed pretty straight forward. Carlos was going to pick up Ruth, outside of a supermarket, that happened to be on the opposite side of the street. All Carlos had to do was get to the other side, park on the curbside pickup spots, and wait for Ruth and her grocery bags to hop in.

Carlos pulled over at the corner opposite the store, pressed on the app in his phone that he had arrived and opened both the van doors.

Back at the party

"I...I fucking love it!" said Luis Filipe and went to grab on to Michelangelo's arm. "You, my friend, you are the future. It is people like you who make real change here in the Valley. I love America and cryptocurrency!"

Michelangelo chuckled. "Oh, thanks. I mean, I'm just doing my job."

"Very good job," said Luis Filipe. "So, what do you want? What kind of investment are you looking for? Are you hiring?"

"Yeah," added John. "Are you hiring?"

Is this my way out?

"Luis Filipe, is that right?" asked Michelangelo.

"Yes, correct, good man."

"Okay, let's do this then," Michelangelo continued. "Add me on LinkedIn, and we can go from there. If you really want to do this, I'm sure we could figure something out. And you seem like a man of passion. Someone who gets and understands what it takes to be successful."

"Awesome," said Luis Filipe excitedly. "I'll add you."

"Great!" said John. "What's your LinkedIn, Michelangelo?"

Back in the ride share, five minutes later

"Where is this woman Ruth?" said Carlos audibly enough so that John and Kim could hear.

She's never going to find us here!

They were on the wrong side of the street, the sun had set leaving streetlamp-lit darkness behind, and the woman's name indicated old age. Things were not looking up in the "let's get Ruth to the van" department.

"Is that her over there?" asked John, pointing to an older lady across the street with grocery bags at her feet staring at her bright-lit phone.

Kim glanced over but then went back to looking at her phone. She started to move her leg in fast-controlled motions.

"Is it?" said Carlos. "I cannot see that far. I think I'm in the correct spot. It says so here on the phone."

John peeped at Carlos's phone from over his shoulder. Carlos pressed a couple of buttons that opened up a chat client, where he picked one of the predetermined phrases

-I'm here, where are you?

Seconds later, the phone got a new message.

-I'm here too. I don't see you. Are you sure you're here?

Carlos replied, *-I don't see you. Let me call.*

I can't fucking believe my eyes.

Carlos pressed the buttons on the app that would connect him to Ruth. His phone's sound played through the car's audio system, to John's torture. He would have to sit there and listen to these two people battle it out over the phone until they finally found each other.

"Hello?" answered a sweet voice. "Where the fuck are you? I'm outside the grocery store. It's cold, and I want to go home. My fish is gonna get spoiled. It says here black Honda Odyssey, which I think is a van. There is no van, let alone a black one."

"Hey, Ruth? I'm here, I see the grocery store. Do you see us? I can't see you," said Carlos.

"I can't see you either, that's what I just said!" she yelled back through the phone.

"We're here, in a black van. The doors are open. You should see the light from the inside."

"I'm fucking seventy-five years old, and I have my glasses to look at my phone. I can't see very far. Can you just come here in front of the store?"

"I see the store."

I'm going to kill both of them.

At this point, John was sure that the woman standing outside the grocery store on the other side of the street was the target. He decided to intervene.

"Ma'am, we're on the other side of the street," said John. "Not in front of the store."

"Who is this? Who's talking to me?" she said.

"It's John, ma'am."

"I don't want John. I want Carlos, in a black van."

"I'm another passenger in the car," John said and took out his hand from the van and started waving at her. "Look to your left, can you see me? I'm waving my hand."

She looked up from her bags and looked around. "I don't see you all. I might just cancel and get another one. I can't stand here and have my fish rot!"

John stepped out of the vehicle, determined to cross the street and personally come get her.

"Where are you going, little man?" asked Carlos.

"Ma'am, I'm coming to get you!" he said, taking a step into the street.

"Watch out!" yelled Carlos.

A man riding a scooter, with an over-the-shoulder laptop bag swerved to miss John and ran over a puddle of dirty water, which splashed all over John's brand new sneakers, sullying them forever. The scooter rider was able to regain control and get back in the bike lane.

"Watch where you're walking, asshole!" he yelled as he scooted off. "Check both sides before you cross the street next time, jerk."

John stood motionless outside the van.

"Hello?!" he could hear coming from the van's speakers. "Is anybody coming?"

Kim, who had been sitting in her seat quietly, took off her headphones and said, "Oh, for fuck's sake."

She stepped out of the van, ran to the other side of the street, and guided Ruth back. John was still standing outside by the time they got back.

"Time to go, little man," said Carlos.

John got in the van and went into the back seat. Kim and Ruth took the front seats. From his vantage point, John could no longer see Carlos's phone, but he knew that he would be the last one to be dropped off. It couldn't happen any other way.

"You all remind me of my family," said Ruth. "You have no respect for my fish."

Back at the party

"Sorry, John," said Michelangelo. "I don't think you'd be a good fit for the company."

"What do you mean?" asked John. "I love your idea and I think you have a big future ahead of you. I'm a good engineer. I can be of use."

"You just...You lack that spirit. You know? Like your friend here, Luis Filipe. He's got it. He's got that spirit. I can feel it. Feel it right here," said Michelangelo as he pointed to his chest.

"Yeah, man, he feels it," said Luis Filipe, poking Michelangelo on the chest. "Right here. Sorry, John. Don't worry, man, you will find something else."

"This is incredible," said Carson, who up to that point had remained silent. "Can we all just go back to the party? I think people are heading out and going clubbing or something. Who's in?"

"I'm in," said Neveah.

John looked at Neveah and appreciated her subtle beauty in the crowd. Carson stood only a couple of feet away from her. John wished he were in his spot. He was too deflated to try and make a move on her. It would have to wait.

"Me too. Let's celebrate our new partnership!" said Luis Filipe, grabbing Michelangelo by his back.

"Let's go. Drinks on me!" said Michelangelo enthusiastically.

"I think I'm going to go home," said John. "I've had a long day."

"Are you sure?" asked Neveah. "John, his app is dumb and you're better off without it. I mean, a bald social media? No offense."

"None taken," said Michelangelo. "But the fact that you're counting those guys out just further proves my point for a sense of brotherhood."

"It's fine, Neveah," said John. "Really, I'm just very tired."

They all said goodbye to John and went toward the front of the house. John walked around the party one last time. Most of the people were already gone, and the noise had gone with them, but the smell remained. Low-volume house music permeated the space. Empty beer bottles and canned wine remnants covered most surfaces.

"There you are!" said the host who had greeted him over an hour ago. "I've been looking all over for you. Here," she said as she opened a bottle of room-temperature milk stout beer and offered it to John.

"Oh, yeah, sorry about that," said John, taking the beer off her hands. "Got caught up with some friends. Thanks for the beer."

"No problem. I hope you enjoy it," she replied. "Looks like you had a rough day, but at least you get to enjoy one of your favorite beers!"

The beer was warm in John's hand. He took a sip and contained it well, but inside he felt as nauseated as he ever had. Whatever a milk stout was, John was sure it was not supposed to be drunk at room temperature or warmer.

"Yeah, mmm. This is delicious. Thank you so much!" he said. "I think I'm going to go home now."

"Okay, well, it was nice to meet you!"

John walked to the front door and went to the place where he had carefully placed his sneakers. They were not there. He looked around, to find that there were only a couple of pairs left.

Yeah, makes sense.

He put on some other pair of shoes that fit him uncomfortably, picked up his warm beer, and stepped outside. He walked down the stairs as he pulled out his phone to order another shared ride but instead his attention was taken by another email from his landlord.

Hello everybody,

The fire alarm did go off. The fire department is here investigating, but they believe there is no real fire. They're going to do a thorough inspection of the building because the central alarm went off, so it might take a while for you guys to be allowed back in. Sorry for the inconvenience.

Thanks,

Jane

PS: Please, as a final reminder, dirty diapers go in trash cans, not the hallway floor.

John put away his phone and took another sip of warm beer. It took him three hours and a couple of needle-scares to get there, but John walked home from Outer Richmond.

7.

The clock on the top right of John's computer screen was about to hit the time to go catch the bullet train home. Another long day of work was almost over, and John did not feel particularly satisfied with the fruits of his labor. The feeling, however, was not unique to that day. Overall, the past couple of months had been tough.

He had barely made any progress on his project, or on any of his personal hobbies, for that matter. He had come to the point in his life where he would tell himself that struggling and not enjoying his weekday was alright because he had other activities to look forward to on the weekend.

To try to cope with stress and feelings of despair, per suggestions from Neveah, Carson, and Luis Filipe, John had taken up and dropped many diversions and ways to calm himself down.

Most notably to him, and to his roommate, who was the most directly impacted by it, whenever John had a particularly long or stressful day, with or without reason, John would take what he would call a "bath." It wasn't literally a bath as his bathroom was just a series of square tiles with a shoulder-height showerhead. However, there was enough room on the floor for him to sit and stretch out his knees in a butterfly position.

He would sit on the floor listening to a playlist, or two, or three, from his favorite movie or musical as the room-temperature water struck his body. In those moments, he wished he were simultaneously there and nowhere at all.

On that black-tiled floor, he had time to reflect on what he was doing with his time and why he wasn't any happier than when he was in school. Sometimes he would feel even more helpless, though the number and intensity of external factors was much, much lower.

Crazy how that works like that, huh?

It was in one of these wet and meditative states that John decided to leave crocheting behind; it just wasn't the thing for him. Woodworking and beekeeping were the two next items on his list, both of which his roommate was against, rightfully so. He did find it fascinating how some people could just pick up bees without any gloves or protective equipment.

Turns out, there are only so many new things that you can try before you figure out that your job and your hobbies are not the problem, but something else. What that something else might be, is what young adulthood is for.

But not everything was as terrible as it seemed. His friendship with Neveah, Carson, and Luis Filipe had strengthened to the point of having lunch with them multiple times a week and, if the circumstances were crazy enough to present themselves, they would even get together on the weekends to go to a party or just hit up some bars.

John regularly called home to check in on his parents and the farm. Triad, his three-legged dog, had injured one of his remaining legs, forcing him to wear a doggy cast. Triad was never a particularly intelligent dog, but he was particularly loved. His family owned other dogs, but they all had four legs, which was a boring quality when compared to the adorable and lovable Triad.

"Everything's alright, son. I hope you're doing well over there in the big city. I hope the liberals haven't gotten to you too much! I'm just kidding, but take care of yourself, will ya?"

"Of course, Dad. Tell Mom I said hello and that I love her. I'll be home at some point."

"Of that, John, I have no doubt. Your uncle tried the California experiment once, and it almost cost him his life."

"Dad, Uncle Joe had cancer and beat it, here in California."

"You can't say the two aren't related."

"Can't argue with that one, Pops."

He would remember the days of sitting on his porch year round, be it during the literally freezing days of winter, beautiful days of autumn and spring, and horrible days of summer.

At least back there the concept of seasons was actually applicable.

He had yet to decide whether semi-perfect weather year round was better than having terrible, just heinous weather for four to five months out of the year, a couple of okay months, and a couple of amazing months. Lately, he leaned more toward the semi-perfect weather. Minus the forest fires and earthquakes, but those really almost never happened.

Right?

This week hadn't been so terrible, but this particular day was a let's-go-home-and-sit-on-the-shower-floor-and-call-it-a-bath day.

"John! What are you doing here so late, buddy?"

Oh, for crying out loud. I don't have much time, I can't be dealing with this guy right now.

Adi peeped his head through John's office's entrance.

"Hey, Adi, I really don't have much time. I gotta go soon to catch this train. Is there anything quick you need?"

"It's okay. I won't take long. I just have a couple of questions about making these dashboards look good." Adi, with a big smile on his face, brought the laptop into view and placed it on top of John's desk.

Oh no, oh no.

Then he said, "See, the thing is, I can't get this line to look the way I want it to. It's too dark? You see how it's too dark? Is there a way to not make this line here too dark?"

Adi poked his computer screen with greasy fingers, muddling it.

John vehemently hated this nasty act but was thankful that it wasn't his laptop screen being defiled. At least not this time.

John's eyes wandered over to the top-right corner yet again. Adi had his Chrome view in full screen for whatever reason, which meant he could not check the time. He had the sensitivity on his trackpad to what John thought must have been the absolute minimum. Yet another infuriating act of intentional anti-productivity nonsense.

"You just have to change the thickness of the line in the settings. It's pretty easy. I can just open up the docs and show you where to look," said John, hoping he could get on his way, his blood pressure and anxiety slowly creeping up.

"Yes…I guess you could do that. Or you could just show me? I think that would be easier and more efficient. Can you show me where to go and click?"

John desperately wanted to take his phone out of the pyramid of essentials—his phone, wallet and keys—lace it next to his computer and turn it on so he could check on the time. His peeing and elevator times were being cut short by this disturbance, no doubt about it. By how much, was the question running through his head.

"Yeah, okay, I can show you."

John took Adi's computer and quickly clicked in a couple of different spots that eventually made the line become thicker.

"You have to go on settings here, then click on line thickness here, then increase the thickness until it's the desired thickness. To make it look even better, make the background of the graph white here. And there you go, your line should be good."

"Yes, that looks much better! I didn't pay too much attention. I don't know what came over me. Can I just do it for this other line while you make sure I don't make any mistakes?"

Un-fucking-believable, it's literally three goddamn clicks!

"Yes, Adi, go ahead. No problem."

Adi then followed the steps John had outlined, failing to change the background of the graph to white. John intervened and showed him.

"Nice, thank you, buddy! This looks a lot better. I just needed to have this graph ready for the higher-ups. You know how it is! They like to have simple graphs with simple lines to be able to see things easily." He cracked a laugh like a pig running out of air.

Does he not see the irony?

"No problem, Adi. Shoot me a message if you need anything else from me but I really should get going. I don't want to miss the train."

"That's true! You should go! I know you have a long way to go. Thanks for your help, John!" Adi said as he walked away back to his office.

John exhaled. He checked the time on his phone. Fifteen minutes had passed. He was going to have to run. It had been done in the past, and he wasn't the biggest fan of doing it, but there were no other options at this point. He packed up quickly, scrambling to get all his stuff sorted out from the pyramid of essentials and into his backpack.

He speed-walked through the corridor and glanced at the bathroom as he passed it.

No time. Today is a piss in the train kind of day.

He got to the elevator lobby pretty quickly and pressed the button to go down. He took a deep breath. From here until he got to the lobby, the amount of time spent was out of his hands. Or so he thought.

The elevator took more than the usual couple of seconds to show up and ring open. Under normal circumstances, John would be fine with the current time-table, but today, for whatever reason, his mind performed other calculations: how long would it take to go down the stairs?

Would he trip? Would he mistakenly open a fire-alarm-primed door?

By the time he was done calculating, the door opened. An empty elevator greeted him with open arms. He rushed in and pressed the close-door button.

"Hold the elevator!"

No, God, no.

It was none other than Adi's voice coming around the corner of the lobby. Then, in that split microsecond, he had to string together yet another series of quick thoughts. Was he willing to take that risk? To leave the elevator open to let Adi in and almost certainly miss his train or to close it and just possibly miss his train. Even Hamlet had it easier.

Motherfucker...

He opened the door and waited for his respected manager to come in. Turns out he wasn't around the corner and it took him a bit longer than John had wanted.

"John! You again! Thanks for holding the door for me."

"Who else could it be but me! No worries, Adi," said John as he pressed the close-door button.

He took out his phone and looked at the time. He was going to have to sprint, and it would be close. That is, until the elevator started to stop at every single floor and people flooded in, pushing him to the back.

By the time they got to the ground floor, John excused himself as he rushed past the rest of the employees, bumping into a couple of shoulders and causing some distress. "I'm going to miss the train, I'm sorry!" he kept saying.

He ran out the building and looked at his phone one final time. The train would depart in five minutes. He was not going to make it, not even if he summoned strength and speed from his old high school days of torturous cross-country.

To his right, some fifteen feet away it sat, like the forbidden fruit had once hung from the tree of knowledge, how once a ripe summertime-Russia in the early 1940s looked prime for the taking.

A scooter. A big fat green scooter sitting at the corner of the street facing the direction of the train station waited for John's decision. John's mind raced. On one hand, scooters had brought him more pain and angst than any other inanimate object in the past decade.

Or was it the people riding the scooters? Was he simply projecting his hatred for self-absorbed selfish people into a combination of rubber and metal?

No, it's definitely the fucking scooters.

On the other hand, John had never, in his two months of taking the train to and from San Francisco every day, missed one he intended and planned appropriately to take. He had come close a couple of times but never quite fucked things up so much that he actually missed a train. Was today the day that he would compromise his principles and succumb to the devilish ways of the scooters or would he stand by his truth and miss the train?

Four minutes later, at the train station

John left the scooter next to the other scooters in front of the station and took his hoodie off. He was deadly afraid that someone would see him committing blasphemy to his own doctrine. He hurried into the station, through the tunnel to the correct track.

But alas, it was too late. His ride home rolled away just as soon as he got out of the tunnel.

Well, there goes that.

In that moment, he wished for all metaphors to remain just that, metaphors, as their realization could be a harsh punch in the gut.

He sat on the station floor and blanked his mind until the next train arrived some twenty minutes later.

People walked past him and into the train until eventually John decided to stand up and join the rest of the late-commuters home. He wondered how many of them had wanted to leave earlier but couldn't.

The conductor yelled softly for everybody to get on board.

I wouldn't give a fuck either if I were this guy.

Even though he was the first one there, John was one of the last people to get on. He didn't get the type of seat he would normally get because of this. But that sat okay with him today. He had made it onto the train and was getting the hell out of San Jose for the day. Nothing else could go wrong; he was home-free.

Now that John had gotten used to the scenery of the train's route down and up to San Francisco, he didn't feel the need to stare out the window in silence to reflect on his life as much. So he had taken up a couple of fads.

He had always claimed that he had no time to read in school.

He would say to his friends, "I'm swamped, bro, I really can't get any reading done. If I had more time, I would be devouring novels and all sorts of publications. Truly!"

He had now set a goal for himself to read the weekly edition of *The New Yorker* cover to cover.

Easy enough. I have at least a couple of hours every day to crank it out.

This endeavor was great, for the first couple of weeks. After which, he started to lag behind and found himself reading a magazine that was three or four weeks old and about current events that weren't even relevant anymore.

In the midst of reading a column on an upcoming Supreme Court Justice ruling—which he already knew the verdict of—the train started a sudden slow-down and after a few seconds had come to a full stop in the middle of the tracks.

Everybody looked around and asked the same questions that come up every time something went awry.

"What is going on?"

"Did we hit something?"

"Hold on, guys, I'm checking Twitter."

"Ugh, this happened last week too!"

"I sure hope we get moving soon. I'm gonna be late for my hot yoga class!"

John put away his copy of *The New Yorker* with care. They usually found a way to get all messed up in his backpack—the cover would rip off or some pages' edges would be bent in all the worst ways. He looked out the window into the dark night illuminated by a couple of houses. He opened up Google Maps on his phone to check his location.

Just a couple of hundred yards from Millbrae Station.

"Hey, Folks!" announced a voice from the speaker. "It seems like the train in front of us ran into some problems on their way from Millbrae to 22nd Street. We're going to slowly make our way over to Millbrae and stop there for a while until further notice. We *will* open the doors there in case you folks want to consider getting home a different way. Again, sorry for the delay and thank you for your patience. Millbrae next. Millbrae."

Resigned, John put both his hands up to his forehead and pulled his hair up. He kept it that way until the train stopped at Millbrae. He took his backpack and walked to the train's exit to grab some fresh air. One of the conductors, who had an appearance of wisdom and many years under his belt, stood yards away. John walked over to him.

"Hey, man, do you have any idea how long this is gonna take? Should I take a shared ride home or something?"

"Nope, sorry. As soon as I hear something, I'll let you all know. For now, all we know is that the train up there is stopped and hasn't moved in a while."

"Gotcha…but if you had to guess. If you *had* to, would you say like twenty minutes? Forty-five minutes? A couple of hours? If you had to guess."

"Honestly, son, I really have no idea. Have you checked the Twitter?"

"I have, yeah, I didn't find anything." John didn't have a Twitter and did not plan to start using it that day.

"Well, I don't know what else to tell you. You can go and walk around but stay close. We'll be giving a short heads-up before we are on our way again. You can also take the subway here if you want, but I think we might have just missed one, and I think it only comes every so often."

"Alright. Thanks, man. I hope you guys figure this shit out."

"Yeah, you and me both, chief."

Once again, John opened up a maps application but this time to check how long it would take him to get home. The result—fifty-nine minutes by subway and twenty-three via car. He closed the app and opened up the shared-ride one: forty dollars for a shared ride to get home and sixty-five for one for himself.

I make money, fuck it, I'm going to take a ride home.

He walked with his backpack hanging from one shoulder and sat on a bench a little far from the train and closer to the middle of the station and started the search for a shared ride.

Are you fucking kidding me?

He did some deep breathing exercises that he had learned on the internet over the years to calm his spirit. In for five seconds, hold for seven, and let go of the breath for six more. Did that five times and then looked down at his phone to see the name of the driver coming to pick him up. Still, the app hadn't found someone to come get him.

Honestly, what did I do? Fucking Adi and his stupid chart. How can a manager not know how to change the damn thickness of a damn line?!

He stood up and walked to the end of the station and looked down at the tracks leading up to where he was. Nothing but small rocks and track. Unlike all the movies ever made where the train was a main attraction, he couldn't see any animals crossing the road or anything like that. Not even a rat.

He walked back to the bench. Everybody else had also given up on the train and were outside staring at their phones and then to the road leading up to the station, and then back at their phones. *Also getting Ubers...*but still, no one to come pick him up. He sat down.

Is it because I took a fucking scooter to the station? Is the universe making fun of me? Are you making fun of me? I just want to go home, man. I swear, I'm never taking another cursed scooter in my life.

John had a chance to sit down and reflect on his situation, this being another relaxation technique he had once read somewhere on the internet. Millbrae Station didn't look the way he remembered it the first time he had registered it in his mind. Back then, his very first day of work, the station had looked clean and full of opportunity.

All the people going to work were all content to be taking public transportation and being a part of something bigger than themselves. The long escalators up and down the station carrying them to their destinations, easing their way. A beautiful intersection between the subway and the train. The morning sun illuminated the glass panes of the station and the big aluminum letters that read *Millbrae Station.*

That must have been a completely different station. No one was happy to be there this time. There was no subway waiting to take people away to their homes or their night shifts. There was only a grim feeling of frustration and uptightness in the air. More than a couple of lights were broken, giving way to patches of darkness throughout the station. Not only that, but in John's field of view, which he hadn't noticed, he saw two makeshift camping tents set up in a couple of corners.

Man, these guys are everywhere. They must be freezing.

Then his phone vibrated. Someone was calling him, a rare instance.

"Hello?"

"Hi, is this John? Are you John?"

"Yeah, this is John."

"Hello, John, it's Jose. I'm here to pick you up. We're all waiting for you here at the entrance. Are you coming? I've been trying to call you for a couple of minutes."

"Oh, my bad, man. I'll be there soon."

Naturally, John was the last guy from his shared ride to be dropped off, almost at 11 p.m. He looked up at his building and stared into the porn man's window to see what he had in store for the public today. A white woman masturbating face up in a maid outfit facing the camera while rubbing her nipples.

Very classy, porn man. Very classy.

He took the stairs up to his apartment. He wasn't in the mood to be gambling with elevators anymore.

Then, one of his worst nightmares. He checked his pockets for his keys and found nothing. He looked everywhere in his backpack for them without luck. Then he remembered that he had scrambled to put his pyramid in his backpack to rush out of the office.

I must have dropped the keys there.

Pushing his back against the wall, he started laughing and crying at the same time.

You gotta admit, this is some funny stuff.

He tried doing the breathing exercise from earlier in the day, but failed. In some strange, fucked-up way, he was happy he'd had such a shit day. Sometimes, if the right amount of shit-winds hit his sail, he was able to come full circle and appreciate the nonsense that had surrounded him, how Karl the Fog surrounds the hills of San Francisco.

He laughed it out with his open backpack next to him for some time until his roommate came to take the trash out and let him in.

"Why didn't you knock on the door?"

"Honestly, I don't even know at this point. I'm just gonna eat some shitty frozen lasagna and go to bed. And God knows I'll pay the consequences of eating this late at night and going to bed right after. But honestly, man, I don't give a fuck. Come help me get up."

His roommate looked confused. "Not even gonna take a bath?"

"Not today. I don't have it in me."

"Okay, man, whatever you say. Have a good night."

"You, too."

John performed his nightly routine after finishing up his dinner and washed his face and teeth before heading to bed.

He laid in bed and checked his phone for a final time and remembered what the conductor of the train had told him. So he went and made a Twitter account and checked the train's Twitter to see what all the delaying fuss had been about.

I sure hope it was something terrible.

He found the account and read a series of updates.

"Northbound train 17 has struck something on the track. It is stopped, causing delays to all trains that follow. Expect delays of over forty minutes." - 6:59 PM.

"Police are on the scene. The train appears to have hit a human soul. Police suspect a suicide. More updates to follow. Trains will be single-tracking on the south-bound track. Expect delays of over an hour. Thank you for your patience." - 7:30 PM.

"Police have confirmed that a person has unfortunately committed suicide. The tracks have been cleared off and delays are catching up. Thank you for your patience." - 8:45 PM.

Oh, Jesus.

He closed the app and was setting up an alarm when he got an email notification, again from his building landlord.

Hey all,

Friendly reminder to everyone that even though you are TECHNICALLY allowed to portray pornographic images out of your windows, this is a practice that we heavily reproach and do not encourage. Please be respectful of your surroundings.

Thanks,

Jane

And then, John finally slept.

8.

Exactly a year and a half before, on the roof of John's house at university

"And that, ladies and gentlemen of the jury," said John as he dropped a dry-erase marker on the railing of a small white board. "Is how you prove that this little fucking dumbass problem is NP complete."

Everybody present nodded and clapped, pretending to be world-famous celebrity judges congratulating a mere peasant on their 'poignant, yet powerful performance' on a heart-string-pulling TV show that everyone hates to admit that at one point, if not presently, they loved.

"Very well done, good sir!" said Carla. "I think that's all I have for you. You just might be all set for next week."

John and his friends had been helping each other out for the past two months in preparation for On-Campus Recruiting, which was to begin the following week.

On-Campus Recruiting consisted of three to four weeks, depending on how far along you made it, of strenuous, constant interviews day in and day out hoping to line up a job for after graduation. To the students' added stress and hardship, in recent years, companies had moved up their recruiting efforts to the fall semester to try to get the best talent before everybody else.

In theory, under this method, everybody was happy. Seniors in college who successfully recruit in the fall get a chance to relax and enjoy the rest of their time at school without worrying too much about their grades or finding a job after graduation and companies get to hire the happiest, most motivated, smartest students.

The problem was that very few jobs were actually handed out during this first hiring round.

But that didn't stop John and his friends from working and sweating it out from the moment they stepped back on campus until they finally signed an offer, if any.

With him that night was Myles, his closest friend from Engineering. They found each other at the end of freshman year and were almost inseparable ever since, trying to take classes together and partnering up whenever possible.

Also in present company were Carla and Irene, two of their good friends from Engineering. Carla and John had hooked up a couple of times but never really amounted to much more than that. Neither of them really had the "time to be in a committed relationship."

All four were gunning for the same jobs and were okay with that. At the end of the day, they all knew that the best person who deserved it the most would get it.

"What role is the first interview you're going in for?" asked Irene. "Tech Consultant or something like that?"

"No, that one is on Wednesday," replied John. "I have them all set up in my calendar. Right here." He pointed at his temple as he did so.

"Got it, got it," replied Irene. "What kind of questions do they even ask you in tech consulting interviews? Never really had one, or plan to."

John said, "It's for a consulting company but I think they started branching out to get engineers a couple of years ago. The interview process is pretty much the same though, as for any other software engineering job."

Carla then said, "I tried studying for consulting interviews, like the case study stuff, a couple of years ago when I thought I couldn't do computer science anymore. The big sophomore slump crisis. You guys remember that?"

"Yeah," said Myles. "We are the few who survive to tell the tale."

Carla threw one of her dry-erase markers at him. "Shut up, you weenie. You were the one crying to me a couple of months ago when you needed help with your operating systems class."

Myles chuckled a bit and threw the marker back at her. "Not in front of the gang, Carla. Damn!"

"Anyway," interjected John. "These guys in these consulting firms don't know the first thing about coding. They'll probably ask me to reverse a string or some shit and move on. They care more about your grades."

"Yeah, that's true, " chimed in Myles.

"They might ask for—," said Irene.

"Irene, how many times do I have to tell you? No one asks about those whack data structures that you love to obsess about. No one knows or cares about fucking red-black trees or tries, or dictionaries. They just want to make sure you know that the complexity of a fucking Hash Map is O of one."

Tuesday morning, the following week

John strutted confidently into Campus Career Services twenty minutes before he was slated for his interview. It was the very first one of the cycle, yet that morning he walked confidently into that building. He had technically been preparing for this recruiting season ever since he had arrived on campus almost four and a half years ago.

He was not going to let his nerves get in his way that Tuesday. Like a ballerina whose feet don't fold over, or a pianist whose fingers don't shake, John's dry-erase marker was not going to waver. He was going to go inside that interview room and answer all the questions the most optimal way while asking his own questions to the interviewer, just like he had read and practiced, and read, and practiced.

They eat that shit up, when you ask them questions to figure it out. They love it.

"Hi, I'm John!" he said to the receptionist.

"And I'm Chardene, and my daughter's name is Penelope. Doesn't matter, kid. Just sign in on this sheet right here, with the time and a signature."

"Okay, sure."

Okay, a little attitude!

He handed back the signed sheet to the receptionist. "Done."

"Great." She put the keyboard with the sign-in sheet aside and said, "Just sit over there and wait for your name to be called. Pretty straightforward. Good luck, Johnny."

"It's John."

"Whatever."

John got to the couches and sat down in a comfortable one. He put a manila folder with his resume on the table in front of him, just in case they asked for another one.

There were three other people in the waiting room. Two girls and one guy. The girls both wore formal business attire, one wearing a pantsuit and the other a light gray blazer and skirt. The guy also wore business attire—a navy blue suit with a light red tie; a clip-on tie.

A tie clip? Are these people for real? Do they not know that out in California they don't wear stuff like that? They don't get it. These people just don't get it.

John wore his nicest and only pair of jeans, paired with a navy blue crew neck. He had considered wearing sandals that morning, to go for the full California look, but opted not to. Not because he didn't think he wouldn't impress the interviewer with his superior and advanced knowledge of California tech culture, but because his feet tended to get rather cold. He wasn't like one of those Midwestern boys who wore shorts during the winter, much to the disappointment of his father, his dog, and everyone who knew him back home.

Five minutes before the hour, the doors all around them opened and a series of students walked out. A couple of them exhaled, one sniffled, and the last one stood outside for a moment, smiled, and walked right out of the building.

A couple of minutes later, out of interview room three, a man in what appeared to be an expensive suit stood at the door and held a clipboard. His watch was bigger than his wrist.

"John?"

John looked around the room to see if anybody stood up. The man at the door couldn't possibly be his interviewer. John could almost see the dollar signs emanating from his being.

"John?"

It can't possibly be him.

"Oh, for fuck's sake..." said the man at the door. He took out a pair of glasses from his pocket and put them on. He held the clipboard up to his face.

"John Buntington? Is there a John Buntington in here?" he said.

Well, damn, they probably sent a new guy who doesn't know how to dress. Or maybe he gets nervous easily so wearing a suit brings him confidence.

"Yeah, that's me. Sorry, I thought you were looking for another John," said John.

"Nope, just you, buddy." said the interviewer as he examined John's outfit. "Come on in."

Let's do this.

Back on John's roof, a week prior

On the floor were numerous pizza boxes and empty bottles of beer. Being on the roof was very pleasant during that time of the year, just after the summer break. John and his friends used it as a study spot to quiz each other on coding interviews, the meat of the process they were all going to face in the coming weeks.

As he walked over to the edge of his roof, John said, "Anybody got the time? Is it two a.m. yet?"

"Just about," answered Myles.

"How long have we been going?" asked Irene. "What's that, five hours?"

"Yeah, we started at around nine, I think," said Myles.

"It's crazy to think that all of this might be over soon enough," said Irene.

"What do you mean by that?" asked Myles. "That could mean a million things."

"Well," she continued. "I guess I mean that it's crazy to think that whatever we are doing now is going to basically determine our future for the next three or four years. Where we're going to live, what we're going to be doing. You don't think that those decisions will come until later but then they just sneak up on you."

"Yeah, it is fucking nuts." John paused for a second. "I remember when that happened in high school. All of a sudden you are sending early decision applications to schools you haven't even visited, applying to majors you really have no fucking clue about. At least I didn't."

"Well, at least now you get to make your decisions more than in high school," said Carla. "At least this time, I don't have my parents whispering in my ears their tips and tricks on how to do something they did twenty-five years ago. There's more freedom."

"I guess so," said John, which didn't sound too convincing even to him. "You still have to worry about making that sweet, sweet money. But hey, at least we're going to get paid. I can't wait to move out of here and across the country to where I belong. California, baby."

"Oh, yeah, John, you're going to thrive over there," said Carla. "I can already see you going surfing every weekend, hanging out with a bunch of stoners, getting a dog. You're going to be just fine, my friend."

"We're going to be just fine. All of us," said John. "We're going to graduate, get our diplomas, and live the good life out West."

"Or in New York!" shouted Irene from her seat, pointing her finger at John. "Don't forget New York! Not all of us have the sunny pot dreams you do."

"Fine, Irene, or New York," said John.

"But mostly California, baby!" shouted Myles.

Everybody started laughing.

"Alright, guys, let's focus in again," said Carla. "I want to make sure we cover some dynamic programming questions before we go to bed. Let's try to aim to be done by four? Remember, guys, we are still in the 'pretend to care about classes' phase of senior year. So we all have to pretend that we're going to wake up at eight to go to a nine o'clock lecture. See you soon, Professor Ramamurthy."

Back inside the interview room

"Hi, John. Please take a seat. My name is Santosh, and I'll be your interviewer today. How are you feeling? Well rested, I hope?"

"Nice to meet you, Santosh. I'm feeling great," said John as he settled into an uncomfortable plastic chair.

John had made up for lost sleep time during the weekend. It had been like a marathon runner taking a couple of days off before the big race. Except his large bowl of pasta was also a large bowl of pasta, some fiery chips, plus two energy drinks.

Let's go!

"Okay then, let's just get right to it." Santosh grabbed a black leather portfolio already on the table and the pen right next to it. He opened it to what John assumed was a blank page.

"Okay, John, imagine the following scenario. You've just inherited a winery. This winery has been in your family's possession for over a hundred years now. It started out as a small winery, but through effort, pain, and perseverance, it has grown to be over one hundred acres. You receive an offer from another winery in the area. They want to buy your winery for ten million dollars. Do you sell?"

Odd. I've never heard of a question like this one. Maybe he's just testing my logic first and then he'll move on to the coding questions.

"Hmm. Interesting," said John.

"Do you need some time to think about it?" replied Santosh.

"No, no, I'm okay. How much money does the winery generate in a year?"

"Well, how much do you think?"

"Hmm, given that that man...or woman...is offering me ten million dollars for the whole thing, then I'd say a quarter of that so that he, she!, would make back their investment in three years. Four years? Three years?"

Santosh wrote things down on his notepad.

"Okay," said John "I'm going to say that the winery makes two hundred and fifty thousand a year."

"And how did you come about that number?" asked Santosh rather excitedly.

"What I just said and some intuition."

Santosh laid back in his chair and wrote more things down on his paper.

John asked, "And how much does it cost to operate? My guess is twenty thousand a year."

"Your guess is as good as my guess," said Santosh, keeping his eyes glued to his paper.

John gave the question some thought.

"Sell it!" he said after a couple of seconds.

"Sell it?" asked Santosh, looking up from his paper. "Just sell it?"

"Yeah, sell it! I don't even like wine!" John forced laughter out.

Santosh did not laugh.

Back on John's roof, a week prior, five minutes after the last time

"So there I am," said Myles, "minding my own fucking business. Our shift registers are all fucked up and nothing is working. We have a spinning row of LEDs that show nothing, and this fucker Will...She—"

"She?" asked Irene.

"It's a him, Irene," said Carla.

"No, Carla, Will She," replied Myles.

"Will she what?" asked Carla.

"No, Will She. That's his name," said Myles.

"Whose name?" said Carla.

Myles started to lose his patience. "His name. His name is Will She. It's this fucking kid from Engineering."

"That's his name? Will She?" said Carla. "Are you sure he wasn't just fucking with you?

"Carla," said John. "That is his name. It's a dumb fucking name, but that's his name. Will She. Now, can we move on? He hasn't even gotten to the good part of the story. Will you let him move on?"

Back in the interview room

"Okay, John…"

There was a moment of complete silence. There were no writings anywhere in the room, no clue that would help him decipher what the fuck had just happened there.

Was I supposed to put the fucking acres in a Hash Map? But that doesn't make any sense. Maybe a Heap? Most productive acres to the top and least productive acres to the bottom? But then…what?

Santosh read over John's resume one more time. John had an impressive resume. Scoring a high 3.8 GPA, all sorts of clubs and organizations, and a passionate cover letter attached to it as to why he wanted to start work and be the best he could be. He exhaled.

"Okay, how about we try something else then?" asked Santosh.

"Sure, hit me with it. I'm ready." He wasn't but there was nothing he could do about it now.

"Your local grocery store, *Goodies*, has hired you to find out whether they should offer a credit card to its customers. What do you do?"

What in the fuck kind of name is Goodies for a store?

John tried to buy himself some time.

"What kind of name is *Goodies* for a store? What do they sell there? Maybe some goods?"

"Was that a rhetorical question or do you actually want to know?"

"I...actually want to...know?" tried John.

"Okay, well, they sell all sorts of things, from food and perishables, to appliances and electronics. They recently started selling a small inventory of office furniture."

"Well, what do other stores in the area do? Do they have credit cards?"

"Some do and some don't."

"Which ones are doing better?"

"Define better," said Santosh as he swung his heavy pen back and forth on the back of his thumb.

Is he fucking serious?

"The ones that are making more money, I guess. The ones that treat their employees with dignity." John instantly regretted inserting his small, yet seemingly controversial, socialist agenda into his sentence.

"Some of them do and some don't."

John thought about the question, and his eyes brightened after a bit.

I got him now. He wants questions, I can give him questions.

"Well, how did the other stores figure out whether they should have a store credit card? How did they do it over at *Foodies*?

Santosh exhaled audibly.

Back on John's roof

"Let me guess," said Carla. "This guy Will You is Will She's cousin. Is that the big joke?"

"For fuck's sake, Carla," said Irene.

Carla laughed at herself alone. This was not the first time in the group's experience that Carla did this, and it didn't bother anybody.

"Just continue, Myles," said John. "Tell everybody about Will's sins."

"Gladly," continued Myles. "So there we are, John and I, sleep deprived, with our heads buried into this thing, happy that it's finally fucking spinning at a constant rate. Happy that we were able to get all the circuitry and shit inside the LED strip without unbalancing the contraption. Finally, we were getting somewhere."

"Fuck, yeah, we were!" said John, who at this point had just finished his sixth bottle of beer for the night. All IPAs.

"And then," said Myles with emphasis, "this fucking guy Will shows up and says to us, he says, he says, *'Whoa, what's that little project you got there? A fan? A nice fan? Are you guys hot?'* He looks at me in the eye, then at John. Neither of us laugh, but he does. He gives us that fucked-up distorted grin of his and walks away, stepping on the front of his toes last. You know, like this."

Myles stood up and walked around, making sure to notice-ably lift his feet off lastly by the toes.

"The audacity! The audacity of Will She!" said John. "I swear to fuck we almost stood up and jammed the damn thing in his mouth and fucked up his smile even more."

"Yeah, we should have done it," said Myles. "You don't fuck with sleep-deprived engineers, you just don't."

Myles was about John's height, around 5' 8", and neither he nor John had particularly strong builds. They considered themselves, in fact, weak. John had done his very first pull-up not even a month ago.

"Yeah, we would have fucked him up," said John. Then he let out a belch in operatic fashion.

"Very nice, boys," said Irene. "Let's get you two to bed. I think we've had enough for today."

"Think of Professor Ramamurthy, you heathens!" said Carla.

Back in the interview room

"I'm sorry, Santosh, I just don't think I understand the types of questions you're asking me. I'm more of a technical guy."

"As a matter of fact, I used to be an engineer back in the day."

He's not an Engineer anymore?

Santosh continued, "Let me think…"

More silence in the room.

Santosh smiled eerily. "Okay, I have a question for you."

Let's. Go.

"Can you code the basic data structure of a Red Black Tree?" he asked, picking up John's resume, scanning the very bottom of it carefully. "In...let's see...you program in OCaml? In OCaml then. Thanks."

Fuck you, Irene.

Four minutes later in the waiting room

John walked out of the interview room puzzled and mopey. He walked with his head down straight through the couches and passed the front desk.

"How did it go, Johnny? Well, I assume?" said Chardene.

John stopped in his tracks and placed both his fists on the counter. He held himself together for the most part.

"It's John, Chardeeeene. It's John. Not Johnny, not Jonathan, not J, not Jesus Christ or whatever other name you want to call me. John."

"And I'm Chardene. Have a good day, kid!"

At noon that very same day

John, Myles, Carla, and Irene gathered at a table in the cafeteria. This had been the plan from the beginning. Go to their morning interviews, rendezvous, and compare questions.

John retold his entire interview process to them.

"I mean, like, what the fuck was that?" asked John. "That was the whackest technical interview I've had."

Myles was perplexed. "What was the name of the company again?"

"Red Stone Co, or something like that."

Carla typed away on his phone and then started laughing.

"John, you goddamn fool, it's Red Stone Consulting! Not Red Stone Co. You just went to some fucking consulting interview."

John groaned. "Fuck me, man. Yeah…that makes sense." He checked his mental calendar. "I remember now, actually. I think I applied for their tech consulting job."

"I guess they don't just ask the same shit now as they do for software engineering jobs," said Irene. "Do they, John?"

"I guess they fucking don't, Irene," he replied and slowly cracked a smile. "But that's alright, that was just the beginning. All the sunny California interviews are up next. I'll be sailing away in the Pacific before you guys know it."

Then he took out his phone and started typing out what he remembered to be his schedule for the coming weeks. As it turned out, he had remembered all of his other interviews correctly. As he was finishing up writing them out, he received an email. It was from his Graduate Assistant.

Hey, guys,

I know you all are super busy with OCR and other things like confessing to your loved one you've had feelings for them, but please, for the love of a God who doesn't even exist, please, make sure you take your number TWOs in the toilet and your number ONEs in the urinals. In fact, I'll make it easy. You can take your number ONEs in the toilet too. I guess the only real rule is no number TWOs in the urinal. I don't care how drunk you are, or how high, really, I couldn't care less. Just please be sensitive to those of us who know how to properly use the facilities. Thank you.

All love and remember to use protection!

Smitty

PS: Remember that Donuts and Condoms office hours are happening in my room from 5-6 p.m. today. I'd love to see your lovely faces. Even whoever committed the atrocity.

9.

Suresh's cubicle, 11 a.m., the day after the train shitshow

"And that is how the rest of my day went, Suresh. I honestly couldn't fucking believe it. It's as if someone scripted that shit," said John.

Suresh sat on his office chair, leaned back sipping on a cup of coffee, feet on top of his small iron storage shelf. John had been retelling him the long unintended adventure he'd had the day before, also with a cup of coffee.

"Yeah, man, that is crazy," said Suresh. "I caught the four o'clock train and got home before six. It was beautiful. You should have been there."

John slapped Suresh's foot off the shelf, making him swivel in his office chair.

"Yeah, alright," said John. "The worst part of it is that I lost the goddamn key to my apartment. I thought I left it here in my rush to get to the train, but I couldn't find it this morning."

"Oh, shit, how will you get home tonight?" asked Suresh, putting his feet back on the shelf.

"My roommate gave me his key, in case I couldn't find it here so I could make a duplicate. He works from home a lot so it's chill."

"Don't they make copies at the grocery store?" Suresh asked. "Don't they have those machines you just put the key in and it makes a copy?"

John slid down to the carpet and continued sipping his coffee. "I tried one of those this morning before work, but it wouldn't give me a copy right away. It told me to pay in advance and that they would then send the copy to my house in three-to-five business days."

Suresh replied, "Completely not suspicious that a key machine asks for your address to give you a copy of the key to that address."

John nodded in agreement. "Yeah, here's the address to the key that I'm giving you full access to. Not even Facebook pulls privacy. I found this place on Google Maps that looks promising. It's called the Key Boss of San Jose. Looks pretty legit."

John showed Suresh the street view of the place from his phone.

"Yeah, it does. You should give them a call."

John copied the phone number from the maps application and dialed. No human picked up the phone, but an answering machine did its job. A raspy, absent voice spoke into his ear.

"Hello! This is the Key Man speaking! I'm sorry I did not pick up your telephone call. I'm probably in the middle of a job. Or maybe I just did not hear the ring, I'm getting old, you see. Don't worry, as soon as I see this, I'll give you a call." And that was the end of the message.

"I'm not so sure about this Key Boss anymore, Suresh."

"Ah, I'm sure he'll call back. I'm sure they don't call him the Key Boss for nothing."

"And some people call me the space cowboy."

Approximately forty-five minutes later

"Hello?" inquired John.

"Hello! This is the Key Boss speaking! You dialed my number? Do you need a key or a job or something? I'm in the middle of a job so I won't be back in the office until about 4:28, and then I want to go home at 4:45. Does that work for you? What do you need?"

A funny thought crossed John's mind. From the sound of the Key Boss's voice, he considered for a second the idea that the Key Boss somehow knew he was going to call and did not want to answer, so he recorded the message just for John to listen to. For some reason, this man gave John a tinkling of familiarity.

"Hey, my name is John and I lost, well, yeah, I lost the key to my apartment. I tried making a copy at the grocery store but the machine wouldn't really give me one. I must have a special key or something. I was hoping you could help me out? I think I am able to be at your office at that time."

John was one hundred percent able to make it in time. Because of the events of the previous day, he felt no obligation whatsoever to stay the full allotted eight hours. He would merrily leave work early to go meet the most interesting man in San Jose, the Key Boss.

"Those machines are crap. They never carry the right keys. I'll see you at my office then." He hung up the telephone.

That same day, 4:00 p.m.

The walk to Key Boss's business place was pleasant, augmented by the fact that he was successful in getting away from work early without anyone questioning it. Not even Adi.

He got to the Key Boss's place at exactly 4:14, making sure he would not miss the fabled man. The so-called office was really more like a house-turned-office that had run its course and was naturally regressing back to its original purpose: a home. Clearly, the image from the street view he had seen was an old one, of happier and more successful times.

It consisted of one floor, with a neon sign on top that read *The Key Boss*, a couple of side doors and a front door. The place was visibly in shambles. A sign printed using a bare-bones text editor on the door read *I'll be back soon.*

Well, if the dusty sign says so, it must be true.

The sun shined bright and hot on his shoulders and back, and also directly on the building's front façade. John peeped through the door, appalled.

Dozens of packages sat on the other side of the front door, some on old wooden bookshelves, but most were on the floor piled up on each other. Even though John did not read his mail right away, he could not sympathize with the Key Boss and his lack of package-opening. He always made sure to open up his packages. Seeing these in different shapes and sizes, colors and wrappings, he wondered what sort of hidden treasures the Key Boss would find when he opened them, if ever.

The rest of the office was in no better condition. Some of the roof tiles were half fallen, multiple desks in parallel to the front of the building were populated with a plethora of items. Boxes labeled *Keys - Special - 1989* and *Desk Clean 2015* to stacks of papers and notebooks. He could not discern a single flat surface not occupied with stuff.

John decided then and there that no one had been inside that building since 2015.

He moved closer to the left part of the front of the building to try to see if there was a way that the two side doors led somewhere, but again, they both seemed to be blocked. A crack on that side of the window let out a strong whiff of the inside of the office. A combination of old wood, cigarettes, and moldy paper overcame him. The air had a distinct smell of rust, which he supposed was from the hundreds of unshaped keys still in their original boxes. Keys that would never take any shape, that would never open any doors, or lock any boxes.

A sudden sadness seeped into his spirit. He realized that this office, home, whatever it was, reminded him of his grandfather's studio, back on the East Coast. His grandfather, a historian and heavy smoker, had passed away a couple of years ago, a death everybody in the family had seen coming from miles away. He and his family were in charge of going over there to clean out the place. Hundreds, if not thousands, of books that were probably read at most once, longing for a new home, awaited them. John and his family knew that those books had no place in the Midwest. Old mementos of his grandfather's many travels crowded that house up to the brim.

Old Japanese scripts, vintage daguerreotypes of American families, and even some old rusty swords from the town of Toledo in Spain. He wondered if his grandfather looked at all of these things more than a couple of times each. At the end of the day, they had decided to put most of the keepsakes in boxes and into a storage facility, but they all knew deep inside that in a couple of years they would end up giving it all away. They just weren't ready to do so quite yet.

Just as his grandfather had died, the Key Boss would one day die and someone would have to clean up after him.

Jesus, I haven't even met the guy.

John was deep in thought when from the building next door an old man, a young girl, and a middle-aged man came out of a second-floor exit.

The middle-aged man sat down on an upside-down bucket and lit a cigarette. The old fella went out to the street and watched the girl John assumed to be his granddaughter ride a purple tricycle. Families were not commonly spotted in San Francisco, so even though none of these people seemed particularly happy to be where they were, John was happy to see them.

"Hey, man," said John to the man on the bucket. "Do you know what time he usually comes in, if at all? It doesn't look like anybody's been here in a while." Five o'clock was quickly approaching.

"Yeah, I mean…don't even get me started," said the man. He took off his hat and started to twist it in ways it was not meant to be twisted.

He continued, "Honestly, this guy does whatever he wants whenever he wants. We've talked to him about it and complained but he doesn't seem to care. If he's not here then he's probably running some job or somethin'. Did you manage to get a hold of him?"

"Yeah, actually. He said he was on a job and would come to the office after that."

"If he told you so, then he'll be here, but don't expect him to be on time." He put his hat back on. "Even when he is here, his mind is somewhere else, and that's a kind way of saying that, trust me."

"Do you know him well?"

"Kinda, but no one is particularly fond of him." He took out a pair of headphones from his pocket and started watching something on his phone. Bucket Man was done with the conversation. About ten seconds into whatever he was watching, he started cracking up.

John got the clue and went to go sit on the sidewalk. He had made it this far, and he needed this key. He was determined to wait for the Key Boss as long as he needed to.

After what felt like an eternity, an old Audi that would have been the top of the line when it came out, possibly not too long after the end of the Korean War, rolled around the corner accompanied by a cacophonous roar. The man inside squinted, looked at John, and pointed at him. He did not stop pointing as he rolled up to the sidewalk, almost running him over. A calculated scare.

The Key Boss shut off the engine and opened the door soon after. He was one of those old guys who opened the door and left it open as they took care of some final business inside their car, either putting stuff in the glove compartment or grabbing some food or something to carry with him. The Key Boss turned around and put both of his legs out before using his old arms to help himself out of the luxurious yet battered interior.

"Are you that guy?" The Key Boss spoke loudly and with authority, although not yet facing John.

Am I whose guy?

"Yeah, I think so?"

"Are you that guy who called me on the telephone? About the special key? Are you that guy?" he asked, now fully out of the vehicle. "I hope you brought it. I'm a big fan of special keys."

"Yeah…that's me."

John, by this point, had waited almost an hour to see him.

"I'm Robert Miller, but please, call me Key Boss. No one really calls me Robert. Although to be fair, no one really calls me these days except for my clients."

"Nice to meet you, Key Boss. I'm John."

This man has to be at least seventy-five years old.

He wore beige shorts with long white socks that went almost as high as his knees, which did *not* seem like they were in the best of shape, caving in to the center of his decrepit body. Just as the other old man playing with his supposed granddaughter, he also wore white sneakers, but the Key Boss's sneakers weren't as clean as the old man's. They looked like they had been worn every day since they were bought, probably back when Bush was president. The first one.

However, that wasn't the most interesting part of his outfit. His shirt was a button-up short sleeve, with white and red vertical stripes. Only then did John realize that the Key Man was wearing suspenders to hold up his shorts.

Impressive. I can only hope to be as confident as this man is at his age at any point in my life.

"Sorry it took so long to get here. It seems as if the city really doesn't like people like me. You know, the ones who drive from north to south and south to north. These days, all those fuckers, pardon me, all those *nice people* in the government want is for people to go east to west. All the traffic lights are always green from east to west and west to east but never for those of us who go north to south and south to north. It's truly a terrible thing that they're doing. No consideration. I just want to get home after a long day of working with clients, you know?"

"I sure hear ya, boss."

"I suppose if you go far enough east or far enough west you can make it north or south. There's no one road that is actually perfectly straight that cuts through the Earth. But these government people, they want me to go around the Earth hundreds of times before I can get back to my shop. And I've considered it. Trust me, I have. Some days I'd rather do that than sit and wait at these moronic red lights. But then they'd win, and we don't want them to win. Do we? No, we don't. I'm putting my foot down every day when I drive up to these malicious red lights. And you should too."

John had never driven a mile in California. "Oh, I do, Key Boss, I do."

"Anyway, what have you got for me? You said you had a special key? Let me see it."

John promptly handed him the loose key he had been fidgeting with in his hand.

"Hmm…ah, yes, this *is* a special key. Let me see what I can do. I think you might be in luck, kid. I may have a spare of the same type."

The Key Boss opened the trunk of his car, which took some effort. The latch wouldn't budge, but when it did, the trunk revealed a miniature version of the office John had just been inspecting. There were packages, boxes with notes, boxes with keys, and a little desk-like wooden artifact in the middle of the trunk. From the right side, he picked up a heavy metal contraption similar to a hole-puncher and handed it over to John. It was heavier than he thought.

"Hold this please. Let me find your key."

He started opening what seemed like random boxes and taking out keys to compare to the main one.

"You see, they don't really make keys like this one anymore. At least not locally. There used to be a factory up in South San Francisco, but it closed down some ten years ago. You can still see the old, abandoned building from the train, but I choose not to. It's a sad sight. Nowadays, they bring these keys from all over the place. China, Europe, and even Mexico." He looked some more then held one up that matched.

"Aha! I knew I had it in here somewhere. Look, look. A perfect match."

"Oh, wow," John said, genuinely impressed. This man seemed to thrive in madness. Was the Key Boss living life in the correct way? He certainly seemed content.

The man sitting on the bucket, unprompted, yelled, "Ey! Fuck you, Robert!"

The Key Boss smiled and replied, "Fuck you too, Craig!"

Turning back to John, he said, "Now hand me back that thing I gave you. This is an old-timer key cutter. This thing here will make any key you want."

The Key Man closed the trunk and placed the apparatus on top of it. He placed the key on what looked like a ruler, trying to line up its edges to different numbers printed on it, his eyes squinted and focused on the job.

"I'm gonna tell you a series of numbers now. See, these numbers are your key. If you ever completely lose your key, if you take these numbers to any half-decent key man then they should be able to reproduce it for you. Write these down."

"I will, yeah." John took out his phone and prepared to listen attentively.

Looking closely at the numbers, leaning in and spreading his legs apart, the Key Man started reciting, "Two... Four... Six..." He turned around. "Are you writing them down?"

"Yeah, I am."

"No, you're not. You don't have a pen or pencil."

"I'm writing them down on my phone."

"That's not writing them down, son. You need real paper and a pen or pencil. You should never trust these machines. I heard on the news that they get hacked easily. Now write these down."

John, confused, irritated, and still impressed, replied, "I don't have a pen or pencil."

"Who doesn't carry a writing utensil with them?"

"I do carry one. It's my phone."

"That's not a writing utensil. Why are you not carrying a writing utensil?"

"Because I don't need one because I have my phone!"

The Key Boss stopped, took a pencil and a small piece of paper from his pocket, uncrumpled the paper, and handed the two over to John. "Now please, for the love of God, write these down. I'm doing you a favor."

"Fine."

The Key Boss finished reciting the numbers then, recalling the numbers from memory, used the machine to form a new key from the unmolded key he had found in his trunk. He held it up to the dipping sun and squinted his wrinkled eyes. "Yes, this will do," he said, and gave the key to John, as well as the original.

John held both of them up to the sun and squinted. The Key Boss scoffed at John checking the keys.

"Yeah, I think this will do!" John was elated but did not want to show it in front of this man. "How much for the key?"

"Of course, it will do, kid. The Key Boss does not mess up his keys. He may have messed up one, or more than one, marriage, a business, and other things, but he does *not* mess up his keys."

John stood there with the keys in his hand.

"Ey, Robert!" screamed the man on the bucket once again.

"What do you want, Craig? I'm with a goddamned customer!" said Key Boss.

"I just wanted to say that I hope you go fuck yourself tonight, that's all!"

"You can go fuck yourself too!"

I just want to go home.

The Key Boss resumed his conversation with John. "Hmmm, that key is an expensive key unfortunately for you, kid. And this did take some fifteen minutes of my day, and I don't have many of those left. Give me six dollars and let's call it even."

Surprised at how little money he had been charged, John took out a ten-dollar bill from his wallet and handed it to the Key Man. "Here's ten bucks. Thanks for your help, Key Man."

"Let me see if I have some change..."

"Don't worry about it, you've done enough already. Good luck with your fight against the traffic lights. Those fuckers don't know what's coming."

"They sure don't."

John had to run to make it to the train station in time to catch the last express train to San Francisco, but it had been worth it. For a very brief second he considered riding a scooter to the station, but he quickly opted not to.

Not today, Satan. Not. Today.

10.

The following Monday, 9 p.m., at John's apartment

"It's the perfect time of year to go too," said John's roommate.

"I guess it is," replied John. "I'm not sure I want to go all the way out there and only stay for a couple of days. I was thinking of going later in the summer and maybe take an entire week off work or something like that."

John's roommate stood by the kitchen microwave waiting for his seven-dollar frozen meal to finish heating up. John usually went for the five-dollar meals, thinking that the extra two dollars didn't make much of a difference. He would love it one way or another.

"If you wait for the perfect time to go, you're never going to actually go. You should just do it. I'd even let you borrow my car if that's an issue."

"That would be nice. Am I even in shape to go on the hikes I want to go on? I might be."

"Again, you're never really going to be in the perfect shape anyway."

"You might be right."

John sat down on the couch and opened up his laptop. He was immediately greeted by the dozens of tabs opened on his browser that briefly sent his mind back to the SAD project. He cleared them all by opening a new window.

He desperately needed a break from the city, his work, and even his roommate, or at least that's what he told himself. If only he could get out of his apartment and into nature for a bit, he would certainly feel better. The mounting stress he carried with him from the office and his inability to do something about it were fueling the questioning of his self-perceived stoicism.

"Where does one even stay?" asked John.

"Well, there are many options. I've stayed in a hostel out in the town but that's a little out of the way. But if you have my car then it's not so bad. You could try camping there."

"Yeah, fuck that."

"So then your only options are the little tents they have for slightly more entitled guests who can't do real camping, the expensive-ass hotels inside the park, and hostels in a nearby town."

"Fuck it. I'm going. I'll stay in a hostel. I'm sure I can find a good deal for this weekend. I will be taking your car though."

"Atta boy. It's all yours, big guy."

John spent the rest of the night looking at all the possibilities that his roommate had brought up. The hotels were far too expensive for his income bracket, and the dingy little tents were unappealing to say the least. He had never gone camping, but he thought that if he ever did, he would want to do it of his own accord, going through the whole experience. Most of them were booked up anyway.

If I'm going to have an awful night, I might as well be the author of it.

A hostel was the best option, without a doubt. It was not very pricey, and the temptation of the possibility of meeting interesting people, as he had done in previous hostels, was too irresistible. He booked a cot in a nearby town for less than sixty dollars a night. Back in the Midwest, that probably would have been enough to book a massive room at a four star hotel.

The drive from the hostel to Yosemite Valley was a little over forty-five minutes, but that really did not bother him. He was not planning on going on any of the day-long hikes, such as Half Dome. He had a different trail in mind.

Or maybe he wouldn't hike at all, and would just walk around the outer loop of the valley. The options were innumerable. John did list out all the possible itineraries he could follow. There were fifty-seven, but they all started the same way. Leave San Francisco by noon on Friday—take half the day off and work from home—and get to the hostel by 5 p.m.

I'm sure Adi will understand. There's no doubt in my mind.

Friday, 9:30 p.m., at the Tree Grove Inn

John took a backpack and a pair of hiking boots from the trunk of his roommate's car and headed indoors. It was night time, and a cold chill permeated the air outside the hostel. Once inside, the warmth of a fireplace in the middle of the main room and lively conversations happening all around replaced the chill and darkness.

"Hi there! Welcome to the Tree Grove Inn. You must be John?" asked a friendly-looking woman with long silver hair. She took off her glasses and dropped them to hang on her neck from a rusty pearl necklace.

"Hey, yeah, how'd you know it was me?"

"You're our last guest for the night! We were worried you weren't going to be able to find us this late at night."

Okay, first of all, it's not even that fucking late.

"Well, I made it, and I'm happy to be here and away from the city."

"You're visiting us from San Francisco?"

"Yes, ma'am."

"Well, we're glad you're here too!"

And second of all, it's not my fault my boss is a dickhead who just can't seem to let me go for once.

"Feel free to take any of the available cots. Dinner should be ready soon, so you are just in time for that!" she said with a smile.

"Awesome, awesome, what are we having?"

"Vegan chili and homemade tortillas. My husband Frank makes them fresh every day."

"That sounds amazing."

Third of all, maybe I should be nicer to you.

The following morning at 8:30 a.m.

John woke to the sound of the alarm on his phone, the same one that the phone originally came with. John wasn't particularly fond of its tune, but the idea of changing it into a brand new tone was a scary thought. It was the same one that woke him up whenever he was on-call, which would lead to unintentional flashbacks and unwarranted alertness whenever someone else's phone rang the same.

Today, however, the alarm signified the start of a day of hopeful relaxation, calm, and a connection to his roots and his inner peace. He needed to take a giant breath of fresh air and be one with his surroundings.

He put on the clothes he had laid out for himself the night before, put on the first round of sunscreen, and threw on his water-bottle backpack.

John found the hostess clearing a small chalkboard to make space for what would be tonight's dinner.

"Good luck out there!" she said. "You're going for Yosemite Falls, right?"

"Yeah, I am. Should be a good time. What's for dinner tonight? I'll probably be starving by the time I make it back."

"Vegan Chili!"

"Is there any other kind?"

The previous night, 10 p.m.

John sat in the communal area of the hostel with a bowl of vegan chili in hand and a small plate with a flaky tortilla on his lap. He didn't necessarily want to make chili tacos, as he questioned the integrity of his corn container. He didn't have much room to operate, and the last thing he wanted to do was spill vegan chili all over himself and the wooden floor.

He compromised by using the tortilla rolled up to rake in the chili into the dip of his spoon, and then taking small bites out of it. An image of a cartoon bunny eating a carrot came to mind. The chili was much better than the tortilla.

"Is this seat taken?"

"No, it's not," said John, shuffling a bit to left on the L-shaped couch to make room for the newcomer to sit on the other leg.

"Awesome," said the man, sitting down. "My name's Gustaffson. Nice to meet you."

"Nice to meet you. I'm John."

The man's wrinkled and rugged face gave the impression of old age and of the passage of time itself. His body, on the other hand, told a different story. Defined calf muscles, strong, intimidating, veiny forearms, and almost no fat on his body. Gustaffson also had a long, mostly-gray, unkempt beard longer than his head hair.

"Let me ask you something," said Gustaffson. "Is this your first time here? It looks like it's your first time here. You have that look in your face, that 'everything's new to me' face. Feel free to correct me if I'm wrong."

"No actually," replied John. "You're not wrong. This is my first time here. I'm guessing you've been here before? Maybe more than once?"

"Well, let me tell you, yes, yes I have been here before. Many times before actually. I try to come here at least a weekend every couple of months. I'd say this is my favorite place on this here planet Earth. Zion and the Grand Canyon are good too, but they are nothing compared to the Great Valley of Yosemite."

The Great Valley of Yosemite.

"Yeah, I'm really excited. The days leading up to this I've been looking up all sorts of pictures and videos online. Definitely some scary stuff, like the cables over at Half Dome."

Gustaffson shook his head. "They don't do it justice. No, sir, they don't. Just you wait until tomorrow. Wait a second, have you seen the tunnel view? Have you been inside the valley?"

"I don't think I have."

He hadn't.

"Oh, you'd know if you had. It's one of the most magnificent views of the valley. It will literally take your breath away, no doubt about it. I can verify this fact. Even to this day, it still happens to me. Majestic. What did you say your name was? Johnson?"

"John, it's John."

"John, man. Listen, I have no family, I was born and raised here in NorCal, and I don't have any brothers or sisters. My parents passed away some ten years ago now. My only family is this here valley and every organism that lives within those beautiful rock faces. The trees, the deer, even my fellow humans who come in to hike or meander around. The bears, the waterfalls, the snow-covered plains in the winter. I've been coming to Yosemite since the seventies, and let me tell you, it's thriving now more than ever. Yosemite is thriving."

John tried his best to listen to the old man give his talk as he struggled to get the vegan chili to stick to the tortilla. He kept trying to scoop it up without any success. His rumbling stomach demanded he do a better job of feeding it. Soon enough, he might have to just eat it straight off the bowl with his tongue and gravity.

Yet, he found some room within attempts to reply.

"You don't think that the more people who come here the less special it becomes? Doesn't it become too crowded? At least that's what I've heard."

"Some people might think that, yes. But I have no problem with it. No problem at all. All that really means is that more people are enjoying Yosemite, and that is a beautiful thing. Hard to beat."

"I guess that makes sense."

"Trust me, Johnson, there's enough room for everybody in there to have a little piece of Yosemite for themselves. You'll see tomorrow just how grandiose it is. I'm guessing you're going on a hike? I'm hoping you are. I've done every hike at least twenty times, and every time I find or discover something new in my journey to the top that just overwhelms me with raw emotion."

John took another bite of his tortilla and flakes fell all around his feet.

The following day, 9:00 a.m., inside the Yosemite's information center

"So you wanna go where? To Yosemite Falls?" asked a park ranger behind a tall desk with a little statue of a Black Bear. The name tag on her uniform read *Hi! My name is Susan.*

"Yes. I read online that it was the best hike to do here in Yosemite if you're trying not to die," replied John.

Park Ranger Susan slowly lowered her gaze to John's booted feet and moved up all the way to his eyes. She had beautiful alluring green eyes that started to pierce John's spirit.

"Yeah, I don't think you'll be able to get up there. It's already late to start a hike to Yosemite Falls, and we're not recommending inexperienced hikers to go up there at this time of year. There's a lot of snow closer to the top, and the cables are closed anyway."

Inexperienced hiker? How can she tell?

"Well, I'm an experienced hiker," said John. "I think I could handle a bit of snow. My name is John, by the way."

"I don't think so, pal. Do you even have spikes to attach to your shoes? Without those, you're going to be slipping and falling every couple of steps once you get to the icy and snowy parts. I'm telling you this for your own good. You should just go to the Mirror Lake Trail or even the Valley Trail and walk around. Maybe you can come back later in the year once all the snow clears out and you've got some better gear."

"So, Park Ranger Susan, you're telling me I came all this way to just walk around the valley? I can't even go up to Upper Yosemite Falls? I'm not even trying to go up Half Dome!"

Again, Park Ranger Susan checked John's look. John thought of himself as a piece of meat at a butcher shop hanging. Park Ranger Susan was his uncle Richard, notorious at home for thoroughly examining every piece of meat he would cook, which included a couple of slaps to check for consistency. John wanted to be slapped by Park Ranger Susan and checked for consistency.

"Pal, people have come from farther to be disappointed even more. Yosemite will always be here waiting for you. We're trying to keep you safe, understood?"

"Yeah, I understand. I guess I'll go walk around for the rest of the day. Thank you, Park Ranger Susan."

"Good luck, Jake."

Every fucking time.

Twenty minutes later

John stood in front of a sign that read *Top Yosemite Fall..... 3.4 miles*

I'll be sure to wave from the top, Park Ranger Susan.

The previous night, at the hostel

"Tell me, dear friend, do you know what the name 'Yosemite' means?" asked Gustaffson, with some food in his mouth.

"No, I don't," replied John, also with some food in his mouth. He'd gotten better at scooping with the tortilla.

"Most people don't, so don't feel bad," continued Gustaffson. "It means 'killer' in Miwok, which is what they used to call the people who inhabited this place before they were massacred by us, the white colonialist assholes who help ourselves to everything we lay our eyes on."

"Who's they? In Miwok? What's that? Some sort of Native American language?"

Gustaffson turned to face John even more directly than before and put his plate down on the wood. "I'm so glad you asked. Most people don't bother to ask past that question or they don't care or whatever the case may be."

Did I just ask Elon Musk to explain to me how Tesla is going to revolutionize the world?

"Well, Johnson…"

"It's John."

"Oh, I'm sorry. John. Let me give you a bit of a history lesson, if you don't mind."

The following day, 10:30 a.m.

John trekked along through the trail, going through all sorts of terrain. He was a thirty-foot truck in a commercial showing the world what he was capable of doing.

He couldn't really see much of the views, as the thick forest blocked it. He did pass a family having a great family moment.

"Madison, let go of your brother."

"Honey, can you just *please* let the fucking kids play for one fucking time in their young fucking miserable life?"

"Mommy, Daddy said a bad word."

"Does that mean we can say bad words too, Mommy?"

"No, Madison, that's not what that means. Daddy is just angry that he is not at home with his friends playing golf, like he likes to do. Every weekend."

Every weekend?

"Not every weekend. Don't exaggerate, Margaret. And for fuck's sake, can we just get on with this and get it over with? I'll carry Steven and you carry Madison?"

"I don't need to be carried. I can walk."

"Yes, Don, every fucking weekend."

"Daddy, Mommy said a bad word."

John left them behind pretty quickly. He had to take a couple of breaks to regain his breath as he was getting closer to the end of that last dusty hill, taking sips of his backpack water tube, spitting out the first couple to rinse his mouth and swallowing the rest. He had seen some hikers do that and thought it was appropriate.

He got to the top of the last dusty hill and patted himself on the back. His climbing shoes were dusty, as was the bottom third of both his legs. But that didn't bother him. He had done it. He had reached the top of Yosemite Falls. He sat down on a rock near the edge and took three full breaths.

The view was spectacular. He could clearly see the Valley Lodge and even some cars driving down the main road of the valley. The forests below composed of different types of trees were all sorts of colors. Bob Ross himself could not have painted a better picture for John. He tried taking a couple of selfies with his phone but they didn't come out great. That was alright.

That last set of switchbacks, a set of back and forth steep inclines, had bested him in a way he did not think possible. The first couple, on the other hand, had gone by like a breeze. John's long legs helped him hike and climb his way through them like a mountain goat, the type that appears as if it's going to fall but never really does.

Ibex, majestic animals.

Two women speaking a language that was most certainly not English sat next to him, no snacks in hand.

"Hey!" he said to them.

"Hey, there," said one of the women turning toward John.

Beautiful, rich French accent.

"What a hike that was, right? I gotta say, I was expecting it to be a lot tougher and it doesn't really look like the pictures I'd seen but this view is still pretty sick."

"It wasn't so bad, was it, Katarina?"

"No, not so bad. Besides, that was just the beginning, right? You're going to the top of Yosemite Falls?"

"Is that not where we are?"

"Do you see a waterfall?"

There was none.

"I guess there are no waterfalls. I thought that was merely a metaphor."

Both the women laughed, simultaneously stood up and started walking in the direction of a previously unnoticed trailhead, hidden behind the bend leading up to the vista point.

"Silly man! It is this way. You are probably about a quarter of the way there. Don't worry, we'll wait for you at the top."

"Where is that name from?" asked John. "I heard you call her Katarina."

"We're Ukrainian."

"Not French?"

"No. Not French."

They switched back to talking in their language, which John now assumed was Ukrainian and went on their way up the trail. It consisted, at least as far as could be seen, of switchbacks.

John walked over to the end of the dusty hill he had hiked up and patted himself on the back for not twenty minutes ago. He considered calling it a day and walking home. The fact that he hadn't made it to the top of the trail did not sit well with him, but neither did the five mandarins in his stomach.

The previous night, twenty minutes after last time

"I see now," said John. "Let me try to give it a shot and recap. So the valley wasn't even called Yosemite in the first place. It was called Ahwahne, and the people who lived in the valley called themselves the Ahwahnechee. And they are the ones who spoke Miwok. But then, the people who would encounter them, because they were so fierce, would call them Yosemite, in their own language, which most tribes or bands of Native Americans in the area also spoke."

"Well done, my dear friend. Well done!"

Why can't I get a girl if I'm such a good fucking listener? Isn't that what they always say in the TV shows? That all you have to be is a good listener?

"Thank you for giving me that little history lesson. I'll be sure to never forget that."

"I'm sure you won't. But tell me, Evan..."

"Again, it's John."

"Tell me, John, do you know who John Muir is?'

"Some nature guy, right? Big advocate for it?

Gustaffson stood up from his chair and sat next to him, practically inches away from his body.

"He's not just some nature guy, John. He's much, much more than that. He had a complicated life, starting back all the way across the Atlantic in a small town called Dunbar, in Scotland no less..."

Did I just insult Elon Musk in front of a Twitter nerd who thinks his anime memes are the greatest thing to happen in the history of the internet?

The following day, 12:30 p.m.

John got to the end of yet another set of switchbacks and, yet again, sat down on a rock to take in the view. This time, the trail going uphill was very visible so there was no room for further embarrassment of the Slavic kind. He had made it there, but the same could not be said for the mandarins he had consumed. Those were in a puddle of vomit three or four switchbacks ago.

He reached a point where he was able to take a good look at the upper waterfall of the two in Yosemite Falls crashing down onto an icy rock. The torrential water crashing down on it made a vast, smoky mist surface all around the rock. If it hadn't been for the fact that it was barely above forty degrees outside, it could have passed as the world's most exclusive sauna. John wished to teleport himself to that faraway rock he knew he would never set foot on and just let the water fall on him and the mist absorb him.

No one had ever set foot on that rock, probably ever. The idea that this untamed rock, most likely flattened by hundreds of thousands, if not millions, of years of constant battering by the relentless water was inaccessible to humanity evoked in him a feeling of grandiosity. Perhaps the only humans who had ever even been close to being on that rock under the waterfall were the ones who had one way or another fallen, willingly or unwillingly, to their death from the top of the mountain.

Killer.

John began to understand the message behind his newly-met friend Gustaffson's never-ending speech. Yosemite brought him a sense of awe and peace that he had not felt in a long time, and he hadn't even reached the summit. The act of reaching the peak itself would come with a sense of peace and personal accomplishment, feelings that he also hadn't felt in a long time.

People passed him every couple of minutes as he sat on the rock, asking him if he was okay, to which he would nod in the affirmative and they would be on their way.

Even though the waterfall's sound almost completely over-whelmed everything else, John discerned some sort of voice coming from a little path different from the main trail that led closer to the waterfall and not up the mountain.

Worried that someone might be stuck down there, but mostly out of sheer curiosity and desire to get closer to the waterfall, John went down the little path. Through some bushes, and a couple of rock hops, a man stood at the end of the road.

"Yeah, that's the stuff…right there."

John got even closer, not sure what to expect from what was to come. Then he realized who the man was.

The previous night, thirty minutes after last time

"And that," said Gustaffson, "Is actually the origin of the phrase *'the mountains are calling and I must go.'* I don't think his sister quite understood the significance of what she was reading in that letter, but we thank her deeply for preserving it for us to read it and appreciate her brother's work. Truly, he was a poet, an environmentalist, and even changed his view on Native Americans as his life went on. A hero."

"A hero, indeed."

"And then began the Oakland period of his life, where, as the title of this period would suggest, John Muir moved to Oakland and embarked on many trips across the nation that would later help him in life as he would stand before Congress…"

My bed is calling and I must go.

"Hey, listen, man," interrupted John. "I really do think I should be going to bed soon. I have a long day ahead of me, and I'm guessing you do too."

Gustaffson and John were the only remaining guests not in their cots. The leftover vegan chili in his plate was cold and hard, the kind that would need several minutes of scrubbing to get out. This happened to him often back in San Francisco where he would be too lazy to do his dishes the night of and pay the consequences the morning after.

He put the plate down and got ready to leave.

"I understand," said Gustaffson. "I just…I just want you to understand the magnitude of the place, you know? What it has meant to me throughout my life? Every tree, every animal, every rock. They all have stories to tell and a role to play in this wonderful, secluded place. They are all working together to make this place what it is. And we have a place in it too. You and me, John. You and me."

Gustaffson's eyes started to twinkle with the dying firelight. Seeing an old man cry is never a comfortable experience. John thought of his own grandfather and patted Gustaffson on the shoulder.

"I know, man. I know," he said.

"I hope that tomorrow when you go into the park you let yourself be embraced by the raw beauty and power of that magical valley. Yosemite. Killer. It awaits you and everybody who will come after you."

"I will try my best," said John. "And thank you, Gustaffson, truly. I can't wait until tomorrow morning to go into the park. But we should both get a good night's sleep."

"Yes, we should."

They embraced briefly and then went their separate ways into their cots.

The following day, where we left off

Damn. He really does have some really nice calves for a man his age.

"Gustaffson? Is that you? What in the fucking fuck are you doing?"

Gustaffson stopped talking and turned his head to find John staring at him.

"Are you jerking off? Is that really what you're doing? Here? In the middle of the fucking forest?"

"Hey, man, just let a man be and let me finish up here."

"Yeah, these waterfalls sure are something."

"I mean, Jack, what did you expect?"

Yeah, he's right. What did I expect?

"Yeah, you're right. I guess this is not the most unexpected thing that could have happened today. But still. What the fuck, man? It's like forty degrees! Aren't your nuts freezing? Do you even have testicles?"

"I have testicles. We get hypertension, not testicle cancer."

"Thank God for that, man."

Gustaffson pulled up his pants and turned his body to face John. "Happy now?"

"Not really, no. I'm conflicted, more than anything. Do you come here and do this often?"

"Pun intended?"

"Intended."

A golden-mantled ground squirrel stood on its hind legs behind Gustaffson eating a nut, completely unaware of what was transpiring in front of it. It munched away and stared into the distance. The sun was shining bright on its beautiful pelage.

"Maybe. So what if I do? Are you gonna sue me, you tech-loving, city prick? Who the fuck even goes down that little path anyway? It's a dangerous little path in more than one way."

"Dude, I could hear your fucking moaning all the way at the top. If you're going to be doing this shit, for the love of God please do it somewhere you can't be heard or seen. Seriously."

"I've been doing this for the past twenty years and only been caught a couple of times. I've had to switch spots and this is my current one. It works, and I have a great view of this marvelous waterfall."

He turned and moved his right hand over his crotch.

"Stop it! Stop that! You are a disgrace to John Muir! I don't think he meant the mountains were calling for sex, man. Just…look, I'm gonna go. You…you do whatever the fuck you were doing here and please, if you see me again, don't say hello, or anything really. Next time you see a young guy eating some fucking gross chili…"

"It was gross, wasn't it?"

"Yeah, honestly, probably even worse than this."

"Amen, brother. Amen."

The golden-mantled squirrel spit something out of its mouth and ran away from the two men.

"Point is! Just leave them alone. There's plenty of YouTube and nature documentaries."

"Trust me, I've seen them all. They just don't get me like the real thing does."

"For fuck's sake. Goodbye."

"Take care, John."

Now he gets it right?

Two hours later

He had done it, and this time he was sure of it. He had made it to the top of Yosemite Falls. There were no more mountains around him, no more hills to climb, and no more switchbacks to hike. There was just a final snow path that led to a flat, rocky surface at the edge of the cliff, next to where the roaring waterfall began.

The clouds were closer to him than ever before. People were eating lunch all over the rocks, happily laughing and coexisting. Part of John regretted having come to Yosemite alone, but it wasn't that big of a part of him.

He couldn't go more than ten paces without slipping and hitting one part or another of his body on the hardened snow-covered surface. Park Ranger Susan tried to slip into his mind, but he was too tired to even begin to contemplate shedding the slightest amount of energy into a love-hate thought. He certainly wished he had snow chains on his shoes.

Eventually, and with a moment of serendipitous grace, John walked on the rock. His feet hurt, his calves hurt, his head hurt, and now his ass hurt too from all the falling he endured during the last stretch. He was still around a hundred feet away from the edge of the cliff where all the sweet views waited for him, but he wanted to hold on moving until he felt better to go stand next to certain death. Defeated, yet victorious.

Something stirred in his stomach, as if his intestines were eating each other and wanted to come out of his body through his mouth. He drank some water and walked quickly away from the crowd present at the summit into a corner. He began retching, wondering if he would throw up again.

"Hello, everybody! Can I have everyone's attention for a moment please?"

John kept retching every couple of seconds but turned to the spectacle coming from the middle of the rocky surface.

A woman stood next to an old man, not Gustaffson. "I just wanted to make a little announcement. This is my father, Jay, and today is his eightieth birthday!"

John threw up a little bit of the recently ingested water.

"He wanted to come to his favorite place on Earth to celebrate, right here in Yosemite. And actually, he just did his fastest time for this climb in ten years! I'm so proud of you, Dad."

The people on the summit gave the old man a round of applause and even a couple of whistles. Meanwhile, John was wondering how he was still able to throw up even though his stomach was essentially empty.

Of course, this motherfucker broke his record.

"Can I just ask everybody to please join me in singing happy birthday to my dad? It would mean the world to him and to me."

The crowd proceeded to sing happy birthday as John sat on a rock struggling to catch his breath. The worst was over, be it the happy birthday or the throwing up. He wasn't sure which demoralized him more. Everybody went back to their posing and photograph sessions.

John felt much better after eating a bit of a granola bar. He packed the rest away for later and decided it was time to walk over and take in the view that he had worked so hard to see.

A short flight of stairs to the side of the rocky surface led down to the waterfalls. Once there, John felt the sheer power and scale of the waterfall flowing next to him, down into the valley of Yosemite. The ground where he had begun his day, where Park Ranger Susan was probably eating lunch, so far away.

Humans could go wherever they wanted to go. Mountains and hills were meant to be climbed, and with enough determination and will, John had proved this fact to himself that day. He finally, unironically, felt that peace, that inner monologue pausing, that he had come so far in search of. The waterfall crashing to his left, and to his right nothing but empty space and a beautiful view.

Parts of the forests all through the valley took on different colors, from dark green and blue to light yellow and orange. Small lines of snow covered the mountains all around him, and again, he wondered if he could teleport to those virgin places and exist.

All the nonsense that he endured at work, parties, shared rides, lost all meaning. He had even forgotten about the haunting scooters. That is where he was meant to be at that precise moment in the universe's time. He would forever be able to remember, and sometimes even access, the state of mind he reached at the top of Yosemite Falls. Inner calm and silence.

11.

———

At the exact same time, 160 miles away, in a basement, below the company building

"Oh, fuck. Oh, fuck. Oh, fuck. Oh, fuck…"

Bob Landsman walked down a long cream-colored corridor at a pace he wasn't accustomed to. He held his laptop with one hand and furiously typed away in his terminal with the other. The terminal kept returning back to him *Access Denied, Access Denied*, regardless of what Bob typed in.

The more *Access Denied* messages his terminal returned, the more he picked up his step, so much so that he had to make a stop halfway through to his destination. He put the laptop on the floor and unbuckled his belt. He then put both his hands on his knees in a throwing-up position, wondering how he had let his weight and age get out of hand.

It felt like just yesterday when he had started working as a security engineer at the company, young and eager to solve all the dangerous security threats that came his way. He had learned back in school how to reroute a DDoS attack. He was an expert.

Back then, there weren't that many threats, so Bob's job was a relatively easy one. No one really cared too much or at least saw the value in hacking into his company's systems. But as time progressed and the technologies changed, Bob's knowledge quickly became insufficient.

He was now a manager of three equally skilled engineers all taking care of a specific section of the company's security. No one really ever attacked through there, so Bob and his boys really had a good time, usually just checking in on systems and chitchatting about the latest sports results.

Bob would come up with the occasional new project to justify having three engineers, but these projects rarely came to fruition, and if they ever did, they were never on time.

Bob and his boys cruised through their jobs.

He was also the heaviest he'd ever been and refused to come to terms with it, wearing pants tighter than they needed to be to work. His belt sat below his belly. Putting the belt buckle over his belly instead would be to admit defeat and he just wasn't ready for that yet.

Bob then realized that he was pondering about these questions at the wrong time. He had to go meet his boys.

He looked up from the floor and read an inspirational quote inscribed in a poster on the wall that read: *Trust, Honesty, and Friendship—The Three Pillars of Team Success.*

"Jesus fuck," he whispered.

He picked up his laptop and resumed his walk toward the end of the hall, where the boys and he shared a control room. After a couple of steps, his pants folded over themselves over the waves of flesh on his waist. He placed the laptop on the floor, again, folded the pants back up, buckled his belt, picked up his laptop, and again was on his way.

Right before his office hung his favorite inspirational poster that read: *You Are Special. You Matter,* in massive black Times New Roman letters with a white background. Someone probably put it up as a joke a long time ago, but it had somehow found a way to stay.

He got to the end of the control room and stood there to catch his breath. He had to make sure that he could speak coherently when he walked into the room to show some semblance of calmness and poise. The voices from inside the room were audible.

"Bro, I'm *telling* you. There's no way he goes to the Warriors, man. You know he's not out there chasing rings, bro. You know he's trying to make a name for himself. He's probably going to join the Pistons or some shit like that and build the franchise from the ground up like all the other GOATs have."

"You're delusional, Mikey. My man is clearly going to go to the Warriors, win his rings, and *then* go to some smaller franchise and claim that he ain't no ring chaser. It's gonna fuck up the balance of the NBA, man. I'd rather the Warriors go four more seasons without a chip than have him come here."

"Now *that's* just ridiculous. Stop lying to yourself or get your head out of your ass, boy. Watch your mouth."

Bob had caught his breath and regained his composure. It was going to be a long night. He walked into the room.

"Oh, shit, what's up, Bob? Why are you all flustered? Did you walk down the stairs again?"

Bob placed the laptop on the table in the middle of the room and increased the brightness to the maximum setting to allow for everyone to see.

"Boys, we have got a serious fucking problem. We really fucked up here, and I think we're all going to lose our jobs, and I'm not going to be able to pay my mortgage, and my wife is gonna kill me. We've really shit the bed, or someone shit the bed. I guess if one person shits the bed then no one can sleep on that bed until the shit is cleaned. I can't clean this shit up, boys, and I've shit in real beds before."

"True, true...," said Michael. "That was a nasty time."

"So what is up, man? What are you talking about?" asked Tomas, as he stood up from a couch and toward his desk.

"We've been hacked. Someone got inside past our systems and is actively taking a bunch of data out. Customer data. The real data. The data that does not belong outside. The data that—"

"We get it, Bob," said Michael. "So you can't get in at all to the DB manager?"

"No, I can't. No keys work. I can't get in."

He unbuckled his pants and sat down on the old, crusty, leather couch in the control room. "I didn't think it would happen this way, but this is how I go. Susan is going to fucking kill me. I can't be home, I need this job. I *need* it, boys."

"Calm your ass down and let's figure this out, it can't possibly be that bad," said Tomas.

From all that Bob had seen, it was.

"It is," said Michael from the other side of the room, looking at the laptop on his lap. "They took approximately fifty million customer records. Their credit card information, their email, their fucking DNA. All of it. And they're going for more."

"We store people's DNA?" cried Bob from the couch. "Why would anyone trust us with their goddamn DNA? It's honestly their own fault. Look at us! We are a pathetic bunch."

"Christ, Bob, you really gotta calm down," said Michael.

The third engineer, Jason, stood up, pulled his hair back and leaned forward, giving the other boys the impression that he was going to throw up. Instead, he delighted them with a single, long "Fuck," so precise and poignant that Tomas, Michael, and Bob, even with his embarrassingly terrible memory, would not forget it for the rest of their lives.

They remained in silence for a couple of seconds.

"Well, is it over," asked Michael. "Have they fucked us and left a tip or are they staying the night?"

"Oh, we're over," bemoaned Bob. "I'll make the call to the fellas upstairs. You boys stay safe down here. I'm sure we will all come out of this one with our jobs, with just a slap on the wrist."

Tomas took a sip of his coffee. He knew that whoever had let the hackers into the system would be fired and they would be fine. Or they wouldn't be. It was one or the other.

Tomas knew that there aren't enough security measures in the world to look out for even the most ignorant of engineers who can easily get convinced to give up information. Someone, somewhere, had been bamboozled enough to give away access to the databases. He was almost certain this was the case. But Tomas didn't really say anything, as he was the youngest engineer in the team. Nor did he care, frankly.

12.

John sat in his bed, the most content he had been in a long time, perhaps since he first started working in California.

He considered his trip to Yosemite to be a success overall. All things considered, catching Gustaffson doing his business in the forest was, at least to him, better than any day at the office.

Someone should put that on a t-shirt.

John opened the window and let the wind roll into his otherwise stale room. Outside, the façades of buildings blushed with the dying light of the day. He pretended for a second that the city wind crawling into his room was actually not city wind, but the natural breeze he had left behind in the Valley. This pretension didn't last very long, as a loud voice yelling from the street saying, "You cannot catch me, as I am myself! You cannot catch me, as I am myself!" quickly shattered his faux sense of serenity.

Then his phone came alive. John figured out from the vibration patterns that he was receiving a phone call. He was determined not to answer, or even look at it. He wanted to relax the rest of the day before going back to work. But then he remembered that his serenity was already shattered. So he looked.

It was Neveah. He had never gotten a call from her. He never really got any phone calls from his friends. If anything, he would use video chat, but never a phone conversation. Talking conversations were reserved for services like food delivery or ride-sharing, two of his all-time favorite activities.

"Hello? Neveah?"

"Hey, John. Are you back in SF from Yosemite?"

"Yeah, I just got back. Why? What's up?"

"It's Luis Filipe."

"You sound an awful lot like Neveah, Luis."

"No, John. Come one now. It's about him. It's about Luis Filipe."

"What about him?"

"Well, have you been following crypto today? It crashed. Hard. Almost every major crypto currency lost over eighty percent of its value. I think Luis Filipe just lost a lot of money, John."

"Well, that is what he deserves for fucking around with shit like that."

"John…"

"Yeah, yeah…that sucks. But anyway, what's the problem? Isn't his family in Brazil in charge of destroying the Amazon or something profitable like that? He'll be fine."

"Carson tried calling him to check on him, but he didn't answer."

Yeah, because who answers the phone these days?

"He's probably just napping or working for his startup, or whatever. It's Sunday night. Leave the man be."

I guess I did.

"Well, I checked out his location on Snap, and it says he is somewhere over by the Embarcadero and hasn't moved for the past half-hour."

"He's probably just looking at the sunset, Neveah."

"Carson and I are going to check up on him, or rescue his lost phone, or something. I don't know. I just don't have a good feeling about this one. You know how much he cares about his stupid crypto."

"Yeah, that he does."

"You should come. He likes you better than the two of us anyway."

Why is she referring to the two of them as one thing? Why are they together on a Sunday night. Did I really just lose this girl to Carson?

"Okay, fine, I'll go. I'll be there in twenty minutes. Just send me the exact location."

"Thank you, John, we'll leave now too. See you soon."

Twenty minutes later

The sun had already hidden away behind the distant ocean waves by the time John got to the Embarcadero. Only a few rays of light remained that reflected delicately off the calm Bay waters.

John had taken the trolley to get up the street and disembarked a couple of stops before it went underground. He got to the spot that Neveah had texted him, and sure enough, Luis Filipe sat on a bench with his hands on his face, head tilted down toward the ground. Carson and Neveah were walking up but still a couple of blocks away.

"Luis Filipe, are you okay, man?"

He turned around with a surprised look on his face. "John. What are you doing here, my brother?"

"Neveah saw that the crypto market crashed and tried to call you. You wouldn't pick up your phone so she got all worried as she does, and insisted we come rescue you."

"She's very nice, isn't she? Always looking after us."

"Yeah, she is. So, are you good? What's going on? You don't look like yourself," said John, taking a seat next to him on the dirty bench.

"John, good friend," he said as he put an arm on John's shoulder. "I'm just—"

"Luis Filipe!" said Neveah once she got close enough to them. "Are you okay?"

"Neveah, yes. I am okay and I am not okay. One can be not okay and okay at the same time and that's okay."

"Well," said Carson. "We should always try to be more okay than not okay."

What self-help book is he reading now?

"Yeah," sneered John. "That, we definitely should. We definitely should be always trying to be more okay than not okay. That is some *great* advice."

"John…," said Neveah.

"What's wrong with you, man?" asked Carson.

What is wrong with me?

All the sense of calm and inner peace had left him the moment he had laid his eyes on Carson. Carson wasn't even his manager or someone who he had an actual reason to dislike. Carson was his friend, a good one at that too.

"Sorry, I don't know why I said that," said John.

"Why do you have to be so cynical all the time?" asked Carson. "For once, this isn't about you, for fuck's sake. Let's just help our friend out."

John thought back to the very first time he had met Carson during that orientation meeting. The only friendly face amongst a sea of nobodies. Carson had been the only person at that table to have introduced himself to him, and John really had been nothing but a dick to him all this time. Well, not all the time but a lot of the time.

"Guys, guys…," said Luis Filipe from the bench. "It's alright. I have seen better days but I'll be okay."

"We understand, Luis," said Neveah. "Just as crypto went down today, it can always go back up, right?"

"I don't think it will ever be what it was," said John in an understanding tone. "But you still have other things going on."

"Luis," said Carson. "There are other options, like index funds, where you can have a more stable portfolio. You don't have to go out and fuck around with crypto."

"I have to," said Luis Filipe. "I have to do crypto. I have to live this life."

"What life are you talking about, man?" said Carson.

Although these words Carson was speaking could have been said by the Carson John had met almost a year ago, they carried differently. Carson was a different man than who he was then. Or was he?

"Guys, I really don't want to talk about it," said Luis Filipe. "I just need some time to myself and I'll be okay. I won't do anything stupid. Just leave me alone."

"I think it would do you good to talk about it," said Neveah. "We're your friends, and we would all be more than happy to hear you out. If you really don't want us here, we'll leave, but I would like to hear what's going on."

"You could probably just give your car back to the agency, or whatever the case may be," said Carson. "Wouldn't your parents help you out if you needed the money? I'm sure they'd understand. People make bad investments all the time."

"Maybe not as bad as this one," said John, trying to liven up the situation with a playful jab. "But yeah, people fuck up all the time. You still have that gig at the startup. I heard too that you guys might be close to going IPO, and you'd be back in the thick of things then."

"You guys just don't get it," said Luis Filipe. "I wanted crypto to crash. I wanted it to go all the way, all the way fuck down. Rock bottom, as you Americans say."

"What do you mean?" asked Carson.

Carson was wearing a good pair of sneakers, and carried a good haircut, a much better haircut than John had ever had, at least in the past five years. John very easily could have gotten a haircut like Carson's, or even gone to buy nice clothes and shoes like he had, but he didn't want to pretend to be someone he wasn't.

He didn't want to buy nice clothes. John had always been that kid who didn't care too much about his appearance. "I can look good if I want to," he would tell himself.

I just don't want to.

Carson now seemed to care. If he had met Carson today as opposed to a year ago, his perception of who he was as a person would be a completely different one. Which perception was the correct one? Who really was Carson?

"I just…ah," said Luis Filipe. "I have never really said this to anyone. It doesn't matter, please. I'll be fine."

"Luis Filipe, come on, man," said Carson. "Just get it off your chest. Your parents won't be disappointed, the government won't come after you for money. You have so much."

"I just don't feel anything," admitted Luis Filipe. "That's exactly the problem, C. Yes, I lose all this money now, then I could make it all again a week from now. Money doesn't matter. Worst case? My parents send me more money. It doesn't matter."

Was Carson that guy John had met all those months ago in that room, or was he this well-dressed and well-spoken man he was seeing there today? Not much had changed. He hadn't gone through puberty or anything like that. The maturation process was long done. The amount of money in his meta-phorical wallet had changed, but that's it.

Is that it?

"Everything is boring," continued Luis Filipe. "Work is boring, stocks are boring, shoes are boring, sports are boring. I try to make myself feel things. Invest large amounts in the most volatile market. Seems like a reasonable way to be scared and excited."

"You certainly seemed cheery whenever crypto went up," said Carson. "Or even with that prick Michelangelo, the startup god. A man among children."

"That is the worst part, Carson," said Luis Filipe. "The worst part. I go out there and try to feel what I think I'm supposed to feel. You know, I read on this website once, that if you force yourself to smile, then you will feel more happy. Right? Simple solution. Smile, be happy. I thought, well, extend that. Pretend to be excited, eventually, the excitement will come. Do exciting activities *and* pretend to be excited, excitement will come."

"No luck?" asked Neveah.

"Man, no luck," said Luis Filipe. "Then I thought, well, if I risk it all with this stupid crypto, then when it crashes, I will feel that pain, that loss. But there I was, sitting alone in my couch watching the stock go down, down, down. And I could not have cared any less. Not even this stupid startup does anything for me. Ambivalence, what a curse."

It's not like Carson had gone anywhere and come back a different man. John had seen him almost every day since they began working for the same company. But Carson had slowly changed the way he dressed, and the way he walked, and the way talked.

John did not believe he had changed. John could go shopping tomorrow, get the nice clothes, get a better haircut, walk straight and talk differently, but deep inside, he would be the same cynical old bastard he believed himself to be now.

Is that really what a person is? Who they see themselves as? Or is a person what people outside of their own cloud of consciousness and experience think of them? Had Carson really changed, or was he pretending to be a better version of himself? At what point does it stop being a pretension and the change is real? You have become who you wanted to be by force of habit. Can that ever be the case? Does it even matter if what the outside world sees is really the only thing that's real?

"And I've known this for a long time, my friends," continued Luis Filipe. "I remember when I was young, watching the World Cup. Big deal in Brazil, big deal. Bigger than Super Bowl, bigger than Beyonce. Man and that guy Oliver Kahn. What a goalkeeper he was. One of the best. This man, big, tall, blond, your classic German. He wouldn't let anything go through the entire tournament. Then, the final, Brazil vs Germany. Everyone was very excited in my family. We had a big party in our house with many TVs, food, better than any of the tailgates I have been to. Me and my cousins, we were only around seven years old, but even my cousins were excited, very excited. I thought, get excited. Exciting things!"

Maybe the change is real, and I'm just jealous of what he has been able to accomplish in one year, whereas I'm just the same old person I was when I graduated college, arguably angrier. What the fuck am I doing?

"And then slow start for the team," continued Luis Filipe. "We had chances but every time *bam!* Oliver Kahn right there to stop the ball. Always in the right place. Then finally, a good chance, Rivaldo with the shot, stopped by Kahn but followed by Ronaldo, the OG Ronaldo, not that Portuguese pretty boy. And goal. Good for Brazil, nothing from me. Screaming all around, so I screamed too but stopped quickly. And then even better goal after. Rivaldo lets the ball through and Ronaldo hits it in the corner, far away from Oliver Kahn. Again, much excitement. We were going to win the World Cup. Nothing from me, and not even in the *Copa Sul-Americana de Futebol* did I feel genuine excitement. And now this, crypto crash. Nothing. There's nothing to be said or done. Not sure what to do with myself. Because no matter what, things will always work out. Or they won't."

They all remained quiet for a couple of seconds. By this point, the sun had completely set and the temperature had dropped. The sound of cars going by in the street had quieted down, leaving behind the faint clacking and thumping of skateboarders in the distance.

"Man, that's…," said Carson. "I really don't know what to say. John?"

"Umm, yeah…," said John. "That's fucked up, man. Sorry that you're going through all of that. I don't think any of us had any idea."

"Luis Filipe," said Neveah. "You should probably talk to someone about this."

Luis Filipe chuckled a bit and stood up. "Don't worry about it guys. Really. I go through phases where it annoys me more. As you said, crypto will bounce back, and so will I. I just go on these long walks and calm down. I'll try something else. Maybe even some cocaine or something. That's what you Americans do when you are all sad, eh?"

"At this point," said John. "Probably worth a shot. Just make sure you can pay the dealer. Maybe wait a bit for that uptick."

Luis Filipe went toward John and hugged him. "Thank you, brother. I appreciate all of you. Gonna walk home now, I think. I will see you all on Monday."

Truly, no one really had much to say after that, and John hadn't even listened to more than half of what he said. Luis Filipe waved them goodbye and walked along the coast north.

He'll be okay.

John, Carson, and Neveah said their goodbyes and each walked to their respective homes.

Yosemite had cleared John's mind and done a good job at it. Seeing Luis Filipe, a source of strength and happiness just breaking down and admitting his biggest qualms with being part of a human experience he did not ask for, would stick with him for a long time.

Also, what kind of fucking name is Rivaldo?

13.

The next day

John walked into his office floor's only bathroom, shared by what he once estimated to be fifty people, holding a cup of freshly made coffee and his laptop. Next to the entrance stood a table used by people as temporary storage while they went on to the stalls or urinals. People placed all sorts of things on it—laptops, notebooks, closed coffee mugs, and sometimes even open coffee cups.

Presently at the table lay a couple of laptops and a fancy aluminum coffee mug, with an open top. John shook his head lightly in disapproval. How could people be so reckless? It was clear to everybody who entered that bathroom that the table was not very far away from the places of business there in the bathroom, and particulates could very easily float over and land on these items. Nonetheless, he moved the coffee mug and the laptops and placed his laptop and a cup of freshly made coffee on the table.

The bathroom consisted of three sinks, three stalls, and a couple of urinals. At one of the sinks, the one closest to the stalls, a man furiously brushed his teeth, staring at himself in the mirror with the water running under his face. This was not the first time that John had run into brushing-man but today, in that split second where he looked at him, he gave him more of a thought than in previous times. Should he also be brushing his own teeth after lunch? He had done it once in the past and felt funny as nobody else did it. Brushing his teeth seemed like a personal experience, one not to be shared with people at his workplace, especially those in the stalls three feet behind him dropping the kiddies off at the pool, as his father used to say.

On the other hand, he only had one set of teeth. Granted, these days, if push came to shove, he could probably get implants, or fake teeth but he did not want to put himself through that inconvenience and associated pain.

As a kid, John was always taught that he should brush his teeth three times a day, but as time went by, the "rules" changed, and the common, society-accepted standard was you could brush your teeth twice a day and have a perfectly healthy set of pearly whites.

But was this brushing-man up to something? Was he aware of a greater truth that the rest of the world was not? Was brushing your teeth twice a day one of those things that scientists would admit thirty years from now that they were dead-wrong on when hundreds of thousands of people of John's generation would come in with rotten, broken teeth asking for implants?

John glanced at him as he brushed very intently and with much determination.

John paraded his tongue around his teeth, checking them individually for any food particles remaining from lunch. He didn't find any, so he decided that they were clean.

Just before the door fully closed behind him, another man, an acquaintance of John's, walked in. John immediately wished that this new person was going to the stalls and would let him use the urinals in peace.

He'd always had anxiety when having to pee next to other people. The urinals were empty, so John walked over to the one closest to the door and unzipped his pants. He tried to rush the deed before the man behind him could step up to the stall next to him.

No such luck.

"Hey, John, how are things?"

John heard the man unbuckle his belt, lower the zipper, lower his pants, and begin laying down a powerful stream into the back of the urinal. John looked over to the man to see if he was supposed to make eye contact. It was never clear in these situations whether or not you're supposed to hold eye contact while making conversation at the urinals. John always tried not to, as it was easier for him to pee this way.

No such luck. The man was staring right at him.

"Hey, man, long time no see," said John, trying to force a couple of droplets out. "Everything's pretty much the same."

"Your boss still being a dick, huh?"

John squeezed out a drop before answering. "Yeah, yeah. A big dick."

John could feel his bladder yelling for release but he was not able to do anything about it. Meanwhile, the man next to him released the Hoover Dam unto this poor stall.

John tried to count the number of tiny, teal-colored tiles on the bathroom wall to distract himself from his own short-comings, as he usually did. However, it wasn't easy.

"Sucks, man, sorry to hear that," said the man. "Goes without saying, but if there's anything you need from me, just let me know. I'd be happy to help you move to a new team or something like that. We're always looking for people over here anyway."

John's face turned red, as he held his breath, desperately concentrating all his energy into the task at hand.

"For… sure," he said. "Thanks, I might take you up…" John released a tiny stream that lasted about a couple of seconds. "…on that offer one day."

Although John was not nearly close to being done with how much he needed to pee, he couldn't stay at the urinal as the man next to him finished up and packed up. Doing so would admit defeat and inferiority. John did not want to concede defeat in this imaginary competition that goes on between all men in urinals, or so he thought, nor did he feel as if he was inferior to this man.

So John packed up as well, and both the men walked over to the sinks to wash their hands, each standing next to the brushing-man.

"It's not so bad right now," said John, still feeling his bladder about to explode. "I'm actually finishing up a project that I've been working on for about a month."

"I'm happy for you, John. It's always good to see one's projects come to fruition. God knows how long they take sometimes to come to an end. You pull and you pull on that string but never really reach the end."

John did a thorough job at washing his hands. The other man just gently splashed his hands with water and moved on to get an automatically-provided paper towel.

Brushing-man, noticing this travesty, spit out whatever minty concoction he had going on in his mouth and said, "Man, don't be a nasty pig. Wash your damn hands with some real soap. That's why it's there."

"Don't tell me what to do. Besides, no pee hit my hand and I barely touched my cock."

"Would you eat off of your cock?"

"No, but you're welcome to," said the man as he opened up the door. "Anyway, nice catching up with you, John. Should I hold the door for you?"

There was no way now that John could go back and try to pee again.

"Yeah, just one sec," replied John.

He finished up washing his hands with soap and dried them. He picked up his tainted objects from the table and walked out of the bathroom. The door closed behind them.

"Take care," said John.

"You too, John," said the man.

John waited for the man to walk in one direction. As soon as he did, John started walking in the opposite direction. He walked all through the floor and even stopped at the snack section to pick up an apple. He put it in his pocket and as he walked past the bathroom on the way back to his desk, he looked around to make sure no one was looking, and went into the bathroom to finish what he had started eight minutes ago. Brushing-man seemed confused but did not question his presence.

Finally, John was able to relieve his bladder in a moment of blissful euphoria.

John again picked up his tainted objects from the table and went back to his desk. He sat down, took a sip from his now-cold coffee, and logged in to his computer.

Today was an exciting day for John. The final addition to his project had been peer-reviewed and approved as of a couple of hours ago. The code was all baked and ready to be merged to the main branch of the code. No more code review comments, no more Git commits, and no more test coverage percentage to worry about.

It marked the end of a long process, all the way from getting the requirements from his PM, nailing down the design with the tech lead, fighting in Pull Request (where one submits code for review) comments with his coworkers about things that don't really matter at the end of the day, but their manager just looked at the number of code review comments. That was not to say all comments are useless, John would rationalize, but a lot of them were non-conversations.

-Are you sure this variable is never going to be null? Can you just add a check? It's just one more line, and it will save you headaches down the line.

-I've gone through every single possibility of how this piece of code can run. It can't ever be null and don't want the code to be verbose. Can you think of one instance where it would be null?

-No, but you never know. I'll approve after you add the check,

-I've added the check. Thanks.

-LGTM - APPROVED

John opened up the portal his company uses to merge his code, MergeStation, and opened up his Pull Request. All the checks were there. His code was going to be deployed to production and monitored for performance. All systems go.

Then, a notification popped up at the top right of his screen. A small banner indicating a new email had hit him. He didn't really get emails anymore, as most people just used chat to directly talk to each other. Emails meant one of two things: some executive was sending some email regarding something not important to him, or his PM was involving a client in an email. He hoped for the former but got the latter.

Hey, John,

Sorry for this last-minute email, but I'm afraid the customer has requested another round of revisions to the application. So please hold off on merging that PR you've been working on. We'll talk more about it during sprint planning, or the meeting to plan for sprint planning, or whatever meeting we're doing these days.

Thanks

John closed the email and his terminal and his browser and ultimately his computer. He took another sip of cold coffee, put the cup down, and picked it back up to finish the whole cup.

"Yeah, of course. Fuck, yeah," he whispered to himself.

And so, John stood up from his desk and went to the break room to make himself some more coffee, because he didn't know what else to do with his afternoon and his sleep problems weren't going away. Might as well have another cup to finish off the day, as he certainly was not going to do more work now that he had more work to do. Out of the question.

John made his coffee and decided that today he would drink it with double the sugar that he normally drank it with. Because, again, why not? To top it off, he added some milk for posterity as well. He made his way out of the break room and to his desk, stirring his coffee as he walked.

Suddenly, John heard a door slam open to his left. Out of a meeting came a young man who waved his laptop at two people and then threw it on the floor.

"I just can't fucking do this anymore. It's the same shit day in, day out, week in, week out. Same bullshit. Of course, I didn't fucking finish. How could I have? Are you kidding me? Are you *kidding* me?! It would have been a literal fucking impossibility. Do you even know what that word means? All of you are a bunch of incompetent assholes, but none more than our fucking PM."

John cracked a giant smile in his face. This occurrence was an unexpected, wonderful surprise. That engineer was living out John's favorite fantasy: standing up to an unapologetically incapable support cast. The difference was that the other engineer actually had the balls to do something about it. It would probably cost him his job but at least he would be free from these people.

"Where is he? Where's his office? This is ridiculous. I'm going to go find him."

He trailed off as he walked into another hallway with two people chasing him, begging him to calm down and come back into the room, while a third person called security on a phone.

John stood there and watched the whole event go down, still stirring his coffee. Two security guards popped up from the staircase and asked John if he knew where things were happening.

"You mean where justice is happening?" asked John. "Where the breaking of an innocent man is happening? Where finally those who deserve to feel the wrath of the lowly engineer is happening? Where engineers will finally not back down to incompetent managers, conflicting tech leads and indecisive PMs?"

"Sir, we're not here for your life story," said one of the guards.

"Yeah, we don't have time, nor honestly do we care," said the other guard. "We were called to come help escort someone out of the building. Have you seen anything?"

"There!" said the other guard. "There's a broken laptop on the floor."

"Tell him that he's my hero," said John.

"We're not going to do that, sir."

"Yeah, that's fine."

The two guards ran down the hall and then turned right, following sounds of commotion. John stirred his coffee a couple of more times and threw the wooden stick toward a garbage can. He missed and did not pick it up.

He sat back down at his desk and thought that maybe he should be the one doing that. But the more he thought about it, the more the satisfaction of sticking it up to the man didn't outweigh the consequences that such an act of bravery and rage would have on his career. Maybe if he had been fifteen years younger he would do something like that. He thought of his wife Mary, and his three daughters Elizabeth, Margaret, and Daisy.

"Nah," he said softly. "I'll just take forever to deliver this shit and nothing will happen. Just ride out the wave a couple of more years and I can retire or do some freelance. That's a thing, right? Freelancing?"

Five minutes later, in the lobby of the company building

"Let go of me!" said John Buntington, struggling with both his arms being held by the guards.

"Sir, you've been pretty aggressive so I'm afraid we can't let you go until you're out of the building."

"I'm calm now! See!" said John. "I'll walk out of this fucking building myself. Trust me, I want to leave just as much as you want to kick me out. I'm done. Just, done. Please let go of me. I'm not a baby."

The two guards let him go. John composed himself and brushed some stuff from his shirt, straightening it out in the process. There was not much to straighten out, as he wore a T-shirt.

"Well, I can't say it's been a good time. So thanks for nothing. Keep your stock, your broken laptops, and your shit people. Fuck you, Corporate America!" he said while flipping off the metaphorical spirit of capitalism with both hands.

"Please leave, John, before you hurt yourself," said Adi from the comfort of beyond the gated area.

"I'm okay! We're okay," he said. "I'm a perfectly rational man just wanting to go home and get away from all you freaks. Honestly, just unbelievable people, including me. I've become a fucking psycho working with and for all of you. And do tell Adam, that bastard, that he's a goddamn loser from me one last time, because I don't think I had the privilege of saying so enough times. And Suresh too. Okay, maybe not you, Suresh, but you too, Adi, you're also a loser. Thank you, and have a nice life, man."

"Take care of yourself, John," said Adi. "But please. Don't come back. We'll send you your things in a box."

"Don't worry, I'll gladly never come back to this place," said John as he walked out of the door into the empty afternoon streets of San Jose.

14.

Four hours earlier

John Buntington was happier than ever to be coming back to work. He felt refreshed, ready to take on the challenges of the week. After Yosemite and the whole life ordeal with Luis Filipe, he oddly felt on top of the world. He could not be bothered today, not by anyone. Not by Adi, not by his PM, not by his tech lead, or any of his coworkers.

He was a new man.

He took an earlier train that morning to work. The beautiful scenes of the rising sun through the mountains and valleys of the Bay Area gave John an even more powerful sense of composure.

The first circumstance to test this newly found strength and peace came not long after John had disembarked the train at Diridon. For whatever reason, people were in the tunnel trying to get on a train going north. John bumped through people as he made his way down to the tunnel under the tracks to get to the exit but nothing serious.

John had a couple of close calls of actually creating events of mini-chaos. The first came at the top of the ramp down, just outside the train, where he bumped into a nurse wearing red scrubs. She stumbled a bit and some of her coffee poured out of the straw's opening, but she was able to compose herself.

"Sorry. Excuse me."

The second close call came halfway through the ramp, where a skinny young man with long black hair tried to get around the crowd and ran into John, dropping his copy of *Dune*. John picked up the book for him and handed it back.

"Sorry, bro, don't try to get around."

Any other day, his own inconvenience at the hands of someone else's selfishness would have caused him great pain and anger. But not this day. John remained serene, even as he almost tripped over a scooter in the tunnel.

Someone ran late and left this here. That's okay. They probably had an emergency at home or something like that.

He made it to work and prepared himself a nice breakfast of sorts, picking up a banana from the break room and grabbing some coffee from one of the machines in the cafeteria. Although John didn't go in early often, whenever he did, he loved it. He equated this feeling to that of exercising. No one ever regretted exercising once they were done doing so.

The halls and open spaces were quiet and bright, with only a few people in their nooks and tables already working away. Even a couple of people were already uncomfortably working from bean bags.

At this time?

He got to his desk, settled in, and opened his calendar.

Today was Sprint Demo day. From what he remembered from Friday, which seemed like an eternity ago, his code was not working the way it was supposed to. But that was alright by him.

He felt like he had labored hard enough to feel good about himself. He simply would call upon the Demo Gods to come rescue him once again. Besides, even if the demo did not work exactly as it was supposed to, nothing would really happen. The company would not go under, his team would not take a dip in importance, and the world would go on.

The more he thought about it, the more he realized the unimportance of his work relative to the massive scale of his company. As much as he hated to think of himself this way due to his abhorrence for clichés, he was, in fact, just another cog in the system of churning out lines of code that had minimal impact on the larger system. In this way, he shared some of Luis Filipe's sentiments. Everything would be okay at the end of the day.

The Sprint Demo meeting started right on time. Everybody showed up with their computers and took a seat at the long table. Everybody seemed to be scrambling to get stuff ready on their screen.

"How is everybody?" opened Adi.

As was tradition in their team, people waited for a long time before answering. Then Suresh caved in. "Good, Adi. We're all good. I think."

"Okay, thank you, Suresh," said Adi. "Let's not waste any time, I know you guys are very fond of that. Me too. Who wants to go first? Dinh, I know you went first last sprint, maybe somebody else? John? I think you have good things to show today from what we had discussed."

Show-time. Or lack thereof.

"Sure, Adi," said John. "I can go first."

John took over the virtual call and started sharing his screen. Opened were his terminal with four tabs running processes, two of which John knew were doing absolutely nothing correct, unless the correct thing to do was calculate wildly inaccurate results for the ingestion of data.

"Can you guys see my screen?" asked John.

"Yes. Yes, we can see," said Adi. "Please begin demo."

"Sure. So these past couple of weeks I've been working on making the ingestion of data more accurate. Usually our numbers are off by a factor of point zero five, and I was assigned to lower that to almost zero. As we all know, lowering that to zero is almost impossible, given the variance of what happens in the process of encryption."

"Okay," said Adi.

"Okay," continued John. "So now, I have the program that calculates the data running, the DB running, as well as the API running. I'm going to hit the API and ingest two gigs of data. Once it is done being processed, the API will return a response of within twenty-one fifty and nineteen forty-five. Might take a couple of minutes."

Everyone sat there in silence. Suresh had been on-call that week and yawned about once a minute, making John want to yawn himself. But it was alright. Not bad so far. His mood was peachy.

Then the terminal in John's screen printed a number of five gigabytes.

"Okay, so it looks like it printed something," said John.

"Does that," said Adi. "Does that say five gigabytes? Isn't that wrong. Very wrong?"

"Yes, I'm afraid it is. I'm not sure what happened. Should I run it again? Let me run it again."

And so he did, but this time, the terminal printed a number of four hundred megabytes.

"John," said Adi. "This is not correct, buddy."

"Yeah, sorry. I don't know what happened. It was working fine on Friday."

It hadn't.

He continued, "It's probably just demo gods or something."

"John," said Adi again. "We talked about this. You cannot just say every time that it's the demo gods. If you come here, and you show up, then your demo better work. It's Sprint Demo, not religion class."

Stay calm, stay calm.

"This is unacceptable," he continued. "We are already behind. What did you think was going to happen? Why doesn't this work, John?"

"Well, it's probably because the people over at Sampath's team have not updated their end of the process. You know part of the pipeline where the data goes is theirs."

"Yes," said Adi. "I know. Did you remind them? Did you tell them that you were blocked? This is not an excuse, you had all the time. It's just a message, is it not? Is there something else you had to do?"

John refused to make eye contact with Adi. There was nothing else he had to do. He had simply forgotten. More than forgotten, he had thought that by the time the demo time rolled around on Monday, the other team would have probably fixed their end of the stick. Not to his surprise, they did not work over the weekend.

"I did not remind them on Friday, no."

"Why not?"

"I was busy doing other things. I thought this would work itself out."

"Trust but verify. How many times have we talked about this?"

Stay. Calm.

Two weeks later, Paula Rogers's office

"So, Mr. Carroll," said Paula Rogers, Director of Human Resources. "We want to be fully transparent with you here today. Okay?"

Paula Rogers's office was on the top floor of the company, in the corner of the building. She had her desk set up as the hypotenuse of the corner walls.

"Sure," said a man sitting opposite Paula. "Whatever you guys need. I'm here to help out how I can."

"So you probably have an idea of what this is about. We know that everybody out there is talking about it."

"Everyone has an idea of what happened, or at least they think they know, myself included. I heard about it the day after it happened and figured that I might get called in here."

"Well, we're just making sure we are covering all of our bases before we make a final assessment of the incident and everybody involved."

"Alright, so what can I do for you? I went over his computer and his network traffic in preparation for our meeting. I'm assuming that's what you want to hear about?"

"You are exactly right, Mr. Carroll. We want to know what he did that day, if possible. Or if you were able to discern some sort of pattern or behavior outside of the ordinary, that would be helpful to us as well."

Mr. Carroll scratched his forehead and crossed his arms soon after, leaning back on his chair. "Yeah, so, like I said, I went through his web traffic and noticed that he logged an unusual amount of hours on social media, specifically YouTube."

"And that's legal for us to do? To look at what people are looking at?"

"Yeah, one hundred percent. If they're on our network then we can see what everybody is doing. Even when they're in incognito mode. I think even in the recent versions of the main browsers they bring up the fact that your employer may be watching you."

"Was he?"

"Being monitored? Not specifically, but passively. Just like you and I are."

"No, on incognito mode?"

"No way for me to tell, sorry. I could go back and look or ask someone else in my team to try and figure that out."

"Okay, no problem. I was just curious. So, you were saying. About the social media use?"

"So, yeah, he logged an average of twenty-eight hours on You-Tuber per week here at the office."

"Twenty-eight, you said?"

"Yeah, twenty-eight. But that doesn't necessarily mean that he was looking at it all the time either. He could have simply opened up the YouTube on one of his monitors and let it play in the background while he worked. I know some people who do that, listen to some ASMR or other calming things."

"Mr. Carroll, we appreciate your input, but please refrain from imparting judgment. We are trying to just gather the facts and go from there."

Mr. Carroll looked down at the floor in front of Ms. Rogers. "My apologies, Ms. Rogers."

"Even still, you wouldn't know how many hours he spent looking at code or anything like that correct?"

"I'm afraid only the online repo's time, but we didn't notice anything out of the ordinary there. We can't really look at how much time he spent or his IDE or anything like that, like you said."

"Okay, duly noted. Thank you for your time, Mr. Carroll."

"No problem. Can I leave now?"

"Yes, you may. I just need to remind you that the contents of this meeting are confidential."

"My lips are shut, ma'am."

"Have a nice day."

Back in the Sprint Demo meeting

"This is very bad news, John," said Adi. "Very bad."

John kept his hands over the keyboard of his computer and remained silent. He knew there was nothing he could say right now that would make Adi happy. Maybe he could try to get the demo to work. But at this point, he didn't really want to and just wanted it to be over. The effects of Yosemite had started to wear off.

"Yeah, I don't know what to tell you Adi," said John. "I'll reach out to them today and see if they can fix it quickly or something."

"It's not so bad, Adi," chimed in Nirmala. "I know the guys in that team. They will get it done. I will help you, John. It sounds like you had a busy week. We all have busy weeks."

Adi relaxed his shoulders and sat up in his chair. He also placed his left hand on his forehead. "What do you think happened, over all? Is there anything we could have done differently to help you?"

"We should talk about that in the retrospective, not in the demo," said Nirmala.

Adi struck back, "Let's just talk about it now. Clearly, his performance is impacted, and we need to do something about it."

"We are not following protocol," said Nirmala. "Let's do it in the retrospective."

"We can start now," said Adi. "And finish in the retrospective. John, what happened?"

That! Exactly that!

"Exactly that! We have so many meetings all the time! We have this meeting, then we have the planning meeting. Nowadays, because the planning meetings didn't go as planned, we have a planning meeting to plan for the planning meeting. We waste so much time! And, no offense, Nirmala, but no one ever says anything useful in the retrospective."

"John…," said Adi.

"If we had fewer meetings," John continued, "I assure you that I would be able to talk to all the necessary parties and finish my work in time. There's just no time for me to just sit down and code! Too many distractions."

"John," interrupted Adi. "Everybody here in the team goes to all the same meetings you go to. We can try to reduce them, but that really isn't an excuse. Dinh goes to a lot of meetings and finishes his work on time, all the time. Right, Dinh?"

"Keep me out of this mess, Adi," said Dinh.

What kind of manager is this bozo, comparing me to other people in front of them. Even I could be a better manager.

Back in Ms. Rogers' office, half an hour later than before

"Please, sit down," said Paula Rogers. "Ms. Gonzalez, from the sweets and coffee section of the cafeteria, right?"

"Yes, that's me," replied a young woman wearing a black apron. "Am I in some sort of trouble?"

"No, you're okay. We just have some questions for you, about the man involved in last week's incident."

"I don't know what you're talking about, sorry."

"It's alright—"

"Oh, wait, I think I know what you're talking about. Is it about a guy who had some sort of freak-out? I heard the guy who came out of here talking to someone else about that."

"Yes… Do you recognize this person?"

Paula Rogers held up a picture of John Buntington.

"Oh, yeah! I know him! John, right?"

"Yes, that's him. You've seen him before then?"

"Yeah! Very nice guy. What happened to him? Is he alright? Now that you mention him, I don't remember seeing him the last couple of weeks."

"He's fine. You used to see him often?"

"Pretty much every day, I think. He would come to the shop every day after lunch. Was it every day? Yes, I think almost every day, he would come to the shop and order one of the big chocolate cookies."

"Almost every day, you say? And then? Do you recall if he would stick around for a bit maybe? Or would he go back upstairs?"

"He would usually stick around for a while. He seemed to really enjoy those cookies. He would also meet up with people and play Foosball or whatever other toys are down here. Sometimes I would even see him sitting on some couch talking to people by the time we closed up the shop."

"And the shop closes at 4:30, correct?"

"Yes, 4:30 on the dot."

"Gotcha, gotcha…did he ever have his laptop with him?"

"Not that I remember, no. I really don't pay attention to what people do after they come and buy from us. I just remember him because he came by all the time."

"Okay, thank you, Ms. Gonzalez."

"Is that it? Can I go now?"

"You may go. I want to remind you that this talk we just had is confidential."

"Oh, for sure. Don't worry about it."

Back in the Sprint Demo meeting

"It's not okay, John." said Adi. "We can talk about it in our one-on-one but this behavior is just not acceptable. You have to be better at managing your dependencies."

"So you've said, Adi," replied John. "We can talk about it in our one-on-one. And maybe I can be happy, and not worry."

"What did you say?" said Adi.

"Nothing. Can we just move on to the next thing? Clearly, my demo isn't working, and it won't work today."

John proceeded then to stop all the processes running on his terminals. If he could only shut them off and move on maybe he could keep his calm. Adi was close to triggering him, but his patience had not yet run out completely.

The room's air conditioner seemed to have stopped working and the air tasted stale, a complete opposite of the wonderful breeze he had breathed in Yosemite.

Back in Paula Rogers's office, a day after last time

"So, you caught him napping how many times?" asked Paula

"A lot. Maybe some ten times or so?" replied Nirmala. "Maybe he was a narcoleptic. That's a thing. I read about it."

"I doubt it," said Paula. "Would you say the quality of his comments on your code was good, bad, or somewhere in between?"

"Well, they were funny comments. 'Check for null here, like my spirit' and 'Did you test this like Adi tested my patience this morning?' You know that kinda stuff. I will say that most of them were useless. Very useless."

"But they were funny."

"Yeah, funny. But no, not useful."

"Useless."

"Yeah, yeah, useless."

Back in the conference room

"Okay, we can move on John," said Adi.

"Thank you."

Everyone in the room collectively exhaled. No one seemed to like the tension that these types of confrontations created. Suresh took off his glasses and rubbed his eyes, and Nirmala finished her cup of black tea.

"Let's talk about Project SAD then," said Adi. "How is that going, John? Hopefully, a bit better than this past project we just talked about?"

"Ummm...," said John, switching his computer to a different screen.

Then, from the conference call system, the voice of the PM said, "Hey, Adi, Adam here, I wanted to jump in just to say that John hasn't sent me any updates on the project or anything like that. I've been waiting for a week and nothing."

Oh, boy, holy fuck. This fucking guy.

John looked straight into the videoconferencing camera through which Adam was watching him.

"Are you kidding me, Adam? I did. I've sent you a ton of emails asking you for clarification on the requirements but I never heard back from you. Do you know how to refresh an email?"

"John," said Adam in a condescending voice. "Of course, I know how to refresh an email feed. I am a PM. You know that right? Do you know how to send emails? I have to deal with customers on my end asking me day in and day out where the product is and all I can tell them is that our new engineer is backed up. I'm running out of excuses."

"Is this true, John?" asked Adi.

"No! I totally sent him the fucking emails."

"Please, don't curse. We're just trying to resolve this. Although, it does look pretty bad on you. I trust Adam when he says he knows how to work an email inbox."

The rest of the engineers at the table nodded.

"Well, regardless," said John. "Adam, you're never available to meet in person. Every time I ask you on these bi-weekly meetings to meet you say you can never meet. Now I find out that you haven't been reading my emails. Is this a joke?"

John stood up and looked around the room, raising his arms as he talked. "Am I being pranked? Dad, are you here to fuck with me and teach me a lesson? Is this all a big teaching moment? You can come out now, you old fart."

"John, please sit down. This is very disappointing. This is not a prank. Coming back to Adam, you should accommodate to his needs. He's the one who is very busy, clearly."

John sat back down, and then stopped screensharing. He opened up the company's employee directory and looked up Adam's name.

"Adam," he said. "I'm coming, man, let's have a chat face-to-face. Enough of this shit."

He closed his laptop and stood up in a hurry. Gasps filled the room.

Back in Paula's office

"Please sit down, we have a lot to talk about," said Paula.

Adi walked inside the room, unzipped his bomber jacket, and placed it on the chair before pulling it out and sitting. "Thank you, I hope I can be helpful."

"I hope so too," continued Paula. "I'll just get right to business then. You're not in any trouble, but we want to corroborate some of the things you wrote in your report to HR and to make sure we get the whole story."

"Of course, I wrote the truth but I'm happy to also tell it."

"So, in your report, you wrote that he would leave work early. Do you have any evidence for that? What made you think that maybe he just wasn't working somewhere else in the building?"

He scratched his chin. "I suppose he could have been. But I would ping him at like 3:45 and get no response. His icon said that he was online, but still I would not get a response from him for a long time."

Paula wrote Adi's words down on a yellow scratchpad. "Please, continue," she said.

"I would even go to his desk sometimes, you know, to ask for things. I like seeing my people in person. And a lot of the times he was just not there."

"Got it, okay, Adi. Okay." She put the pad on her lap and took off her glasses. "So we were able to look at his Git commit history and saw that in his one year here with us, he only opened up..." She put her glasses on again, read some numbers on a paper next to her, and took them off. "...twenty-five pull requests and contributed fewer than ten thousand lines of code."

"Oh, really?"

"Yes, really."

"Now that is an interesting statistic."

"So fascinating, right?" she said in a condescending tone. "Other people in your team usually average over ninety-thousand lines."

"Oh, really? I thought the number was a different number. I confuse numbers all the time. He was a new employee though. I always try to give my new engineers the benefit of the doubt."

"I couldn't have said it better."

Adi looked perplexed. He didn't know what he had said that couldn't have been said better. "What is that, Ms. Rogers?"

"That he was, after all, an employee, new or old. An employee." Paula Rogers stopped her questioning and looked over her notes. "I think it's time we talk about the emails? To his PM?"

"Ah, yes, the mess of the emails. Actually, a very funny story..."

Five minutes later than before, in the conference room

John turned around the corner at the end of the hall and into the utility staircase. He was faster than the rest of his colleagues who were actively chasing him.

He pushed open the door two floors below and looked quickly at a map of the layout of the floor before heading to the precise location of Adam's office, 3-18. He stood outside for the moment and gathered himself.

Alright, fucker, your time is up.

He knocked on the door and walked inside.

"Excuse me, who are you?" said the man inside the office.

"Don't play games, Adam. How come you never come to any of our meetings? Let me see your inbox!"

At this point, John's co-workers arrived and stood behind him, panting for their breath. Nirmala, Suresh, and Adi. Dinh had not bothered to show up.

"John," said Adi. "You're in the—"

John turned and pointed at him. "You shut up! You don't talk right now! This is between me and Mr. SAD Project, Mr. Adam here."

The man in the office shook his head. "I really have no clue who the hell you people are. My name is Adam but I don't know anything about Project SAD. I must say, seems like rather a stupid name."

"You're telling me!" said John. "Stop it with the bullshit, man. You are Adam, Adam Nolan? The bastard who doesn't know how to read emails?"

Adam looked to his monitor and then back up to John with his eyebrows pointing inward toward the center of his face.

"It's pronounced Nowlan, like Now and then LAN, like LAN party. It's honestly quite phonetic. You just have to read the name like it sounds."

"John, this is what—," said Adi.

"Wait, wait, wait...*now*? Nowlan with a fucking double u?" said John.

"That's me!" said Adam, pointing to the placard on top of his desk. "Now would you kindly get the hell out of my office? I have actual work to do, unlike you clowns."

"I am so sorry," said John. "I had you confused with some other idiot PM."

"Aren't we all?"

John walked outside the office defeated.

"John, Adam isn't even in this office. He works out of New York City," said Adi.

John walked past Adi, Suresh, and Nirmala, who all tried to stop him in his tracks.

"I'm done. I'm getting the fuck out of here. I don't ever want to know of you people again."

A couple of police officers finally found John, sulking as he walked back toward the stairs.

"Sir, we're going to need you to come with us."

Back in Paula's office

"So, as it turns out," said Adi. "He emailed the wrong person. And the IT guys were telling me that they found a bunch of drafts in his inbox. I think he was confused as to how to send an email and thought that by saving them as drafts, he would also be sending them or something."

Paula Rogers smirked a bit, took off her glasses, and laid them on the table. "So it sounds like he was a very incompetent engineer. Is that a fair assessment?"

"Uhm, yeah," said Adi. "Incompetent. And angry. He was very angry all the time. Like, all the time."

"What a shame; a bright young man gone to waste. I think we have enough, Adi. Thank you for stopping by."

Adi stood up with his classic big, white smile. "My pleasure!"

He carried with him a worn-out notebook, a pen stuck in between pages.

15.

John meandered down the streets of San Jose for what could possibly be his last time. The next train would not depart the station for another fifty minutes. He had plenty of time to try to process and reevaluate everything in his life.

The hot San Jose sun did not immediately make its effect known to John. The photons it emitted, however, were nonetheless colliding with his skin and clothing, releasing their energy and gradually building up a layer of warmth around him.

Tiny stab-like and itching sensations popped up all around John's body. First his upper back, then on his chest, right around his nipples. He scratched his back to appease it. On the other hand, scratching on or around his nipples always posed a risk. Some days he would scratch them and find relief, but most days he would just end up exacerbating the horrible sensation.

Since he hadn't quite had enough horrible sensations for the day, he went for it. Fortunately, at least for the moment, it seemed to have worked.

He continued down his walk and tried to appreciate the beautiful sights around him. People without homes under the bridge, skateboarders skating through the red lights, construction workers eating their lunch under limited shade. Truly a beautiful scene.

None of those people knew or cared that he had just had one of the most intense, yet liberating experiences of his life. He wondered if they even knew what the word *cathartic* meant.

Of course, they do, you elitist bastard.

He wasn't quite sure how to feel about everything that had just happened. His initial instinct was to not think about it and let it simmer until he got home and was in a more comfortable and safe space. Perhaps he could even call his dad.

But he couldn't help himself.

The more he tried to avoid thinking about it, the more he did. And the more he thought about it, the more it started to hit him that he would possibly never find another job in the industry. That his reputation as a Software Engineer was forever tainted. Adi and his company would make sure to put in a word everywhere that he was not to be trusted or hired.

Now, the question he inevitably asked himself was, was this fact alright by him?

Five years later, in a board room at one of the largest venture capital firms in the United States

Five men and five women sat in large, comfortable leather chairs with thick portfolios in front of them. They all read them carefully and thoroughly, examining the results and projections of their potential investment.

"And it works? Like, really works?" asked the woman sitting at the top of the table, flipping back to the first page of the portfolio, taking off her glasses and addressing the person on the other side of the table.

"Yes, it does. It works very well," replied the man being questioned.

The head of the committee again put on her glasses and flipped halfway through the portfolio.

"So the graph in section Four-C," asked the man to the right side of the woman. "That graph is accurate and has been corroborated by multiple scientific bodies, correct?"

"Yes, that is correct," again replied the man.

A couple of the other people in the room had already closed the portfolios and sat smiling in the man's direction.

The head honcho closed the portfolio and took off her glasses. She stood up from her chair and walked to the window. She looked at the outside world from the forty-fifth floor of the Manhattan skyscraper her firm occupied.

"What you have here is truly remarkable," she said. "Opportunities like these, with this much growth potential and market excitement, don't really come around often."

"Thank you, ma'am," replied the man.

The room went completely quiet as she walked toward the man, the sound of her heels muffled by the carpet, yet audible by the intensity of her step, filling the room.

"Well," she said, extending her hand toward him. "Adi, not only are you going to change the world with this, but all of us here are going to make sure you come out of this very, very rich. Just like all of us."

Adi smiled with his pearl-white teeth and stood up to shake her hand. "Thank you so much. I'm excited for our partnership and to change the world. I'm glad you've agreed to my terms."

"And we thank you for choosing us," she said.

The rest of the board of directors of the firm stood up and clapped loudly.

Back on the streets of San Jose

Suddenly, the loud sound of an approaching airplane caught John's attention. He looked up to see a giant steel beast fly over toward San Jose's airport, no more than ten miles away.

The flying monster gently adjusted its wings, as it prepared for landing. For a second, John thought that he could probably run as fast as the airplane glided in. If his many years growing up playing a flight simulator in his computer back home had taught him anything, it was that those last two miles were the most crucial. It was all up to the pilot, to make sure the plane was aligned with the runway and that the impact with the ground wouldn't be too hard on its passengers.

But then again, he was playing a game from 1995. The technology had probably changed. Planes were a lot safer these days and their computers were always to be trusted.

The airplane went out of his sight and John continued his walk toward the train station. He took a different route because he could. He normally only ever left the office with the exact amount of time needed, so that day was his chance to explore just a bit.

A man riding a scooter on the opposite side of the road came into John's view. He wore a helmet, rode in the appropriate lane, and was looking straight on.

Why can't they all be like him?

The scooter man cruised through the streets at the predetermined scooter speed limit. He looked majestic. The sun reflected off the man's helmet, making him almost look angelic. The last mile of that man's commute would be a happy one, and for once, John was happy to see a scooter. Quickly after that, he went out of view.

Just as John turned back to look at his own path, his foot hit a heavy object, and John went crashing down, all the way to the curb.

I can't honestly, fucking, what.

He looked behind himself and saw, what else, but a scooter. The scooter's handlebars on the ground resembled a mocking smile, as the speaker of it voiced, "Please, pick me up. I don't belong on the ground," over and over.

At this point, John's hypothesis that scooters were their own evil, animated objects, creeped back into his subconscious.

But they were just metal and plastic. Nothing else.

Then why is it mocking me?

John stood up and stared down at the scooter and spit on it three times. He had made up his mind. That was all he would do to the scooter and that the moment he got home to San Francisco, and hell, even back to the Midwest, he would never have to see them again. He was going to let this poor guy live.

Twenty years later, at a large tech conference, Center Stage

"So no one believed it would work? Not even in the later days of your company?" asked Chris, the host, who sat with his legs crossed on a red chair opposite to Adi, in a teal chair.

The two of them were on a stage in front of thousands of people who had come from all corners of the world to see the tech tycoon and certified genius, Adi. Tickets to the conference had sold out the day it was announced that Adi would lead the main panel on innovation and technology.

He wore a red velvet jacket and a pair of black corduroy pants, accompanied with a pair of expensive leather loafers.

"Well, Chris," said Adi. "No one ever started a company with the full support of their friends and family. That is just a fact of life, business, and the world we live in. We don't support each other enough and are constantly criticizing, not with the intent of helping our fellow humans, but with an intent of discouragement coming from a place of jealousy."

"Tell us more about that," said Chris.

"Treating people with respect and kindness is the only way to succeed. I knew this from the moment I became a manager and always lived by these standards. And these are the standards that I instilled in my company since day one. And look at us now."

The audience clapped and cheered.

"I think," he continued, "that the technology we've been able to develop would not have been possible without the trust of those who *did* support me through the years. And of course, the result of my countless hours of thinking and solitude."

"Thinking and solitude," said Chris.

"Yes," continued Adi. "Thinking and solitude. You guys can put that on a t-shirt. It's free!"

The audience laughed and again clapped and cheered.

"We're just lucky to have you here," said Chris. "It's not every day that the great Adi takes the time to address the public. So tell us, are you working on any exciting new projects?"

"As a matter of fact, I am."

He grabbed some mixture from the table in front of them and audibly crushed it with his spotless teeth.

Back in San Jose

Nah. Fuck this guy.

John picked up the scooter behind him and slammed it on the ground. He anxiously looked around for any heavy object he could find.

After a couple of minutes of searching, he found a heavy, pointy rock in an abandoned field. He ran back to where the scooter lay on the ground, yelling, and knelt. He put his ear up close to the scooter and tried to locate where the voice was coming from.

It's coming from underneath the damned thing.

He turned the scooter around, and with utter rage and primal grunts, he repeatedly pounded the belly of the scooter with his weapon. Over and over. The sound of the scooter slowly fading until there was nothing left of it.

John then stood up, picked up the scooter, and once again slammed it to the ground, before spitting on it again.

He felt alive knowing the scooter was dead.

He ran down the street and toward the train station where he knew many more scooters would be, awaiting their beatdown.

Once there, he toppled every single last one of them roughly to the ground. He picked some up and slammed them against others on the ground, all the while dozens of voices yelled, "Please, pick me up. I don't belong on the ground."

No, you fucking deserve to stop breathing and fucking just die.

He continued the slamming of the scooters, removing their voices when he could with his trusty rock. That was until he ran out of air.

By the time he was done, they were all in a pile, with smoke coming out of them.

Surely, some of the batteries were not having a good time.

He stood over his victims, with one hand unzipped his pants, and emptied his bladder on them, giving him perhaps the greatest feeling of satisfaction he had felt in a long, long time.

He walked into the train station, hair and clothes all messed up, sweat dripping down him everywhere. People stared at him with perplexed faces.

He continued down through the main hall, through the tunnels and onto the platform where the train coming in ten more minutes would take him home.

John Buntington sat down on a waiting bench, closed his eyes, and exhaled. He still held on to the rock, now battered, that slowly built up a pool of scooter oil at John's feet.

Now, he was truly free.

Forty years later at the Nobel Peace Prize Award Ceremony

Adi held both sides of the podium and gave the large audience one of the biggest smiles of his life. "Honestly, guys, I never thought, not in a million years, that my work could ever help in ousting and dismantling fascist regimes all throughout the world. It is, truly, my biggest joy to have my work been involved in the last three coup d'états that helped restore balance to the global scale, while also minimizing the loss of human life. Honesty, I can't believe it. I really can't."

He pulled out a crusty old notebook from his jacket. "And it all started right here," he said, pointing to it. "Right here, in this little notebook, a little over forty years ago today. I hope I've inspired generations to come to follow their dreams and know that they can, too, change the world. And as I've always said, if you follow this advice you will never fail. Be happy, don't worry."

EPILOGUE.

One month after John's last day at the company, 7 a.m.

John sat reclined in a comfortable lawn chair on his house's porch, overlooking the extensive and beautiful rows of endless, yellow-tipped, cornstalks.

After his glorious last hurrah in San Jose, he had decided it would be best for him to move out of the Bay Area and go back home to live with his family. So, he packed up all his valuables to take with him and threw away the rest.

He still had to pay his portion of the rent, but it was no big bother. The lease would be up in a couple of months. His roommate did not seem to mind too much that John had moved out. He had sent John a picture of how he turned his room into a personal gym, consisting of a stationary bike. John was proud of him.

John had moved home just in time for the harvest and was actually excited for it. The last time he had experienced it he was a mere child of seventeen years, just before heading off for college.

Every year he hated everything about the corn stages, but this year it felt different.

No one was calling him in the middle of the night, there were no screens in sight, and most importantly, there probably were no scooters in a hundred-mile radius from his house.

John had been looking forward to going out to the fields and operating the machinery to get the corn out of its nest and into huge containers before it would inevitably be shipped out.

His dog, Triad, sat next to him, licking his own anus and the stub of his missing leg. Back and forth, Triad's tongue went between the two spots.

What a blissful existence.

John wondered for a second if he could lick his own anus.

The screen door that led to the house opened, and out walked John's dad, looking burlier and older than he had remembered him.

He held a big cup of steaming coffee and wore a cap that spread a message of support for the local conservative candidate running for city council. "It is good to have you back, John."

"Yeah, it's good to be back, Dad."

"Your mother and I missed you, although I might not admit it often."

"I missed you guys too."

"I do admit it more often than you admit you were wrong for going out and trying to be a software engineer or some stupid shit like that."

There it is.

John stood up from the chair and patted his father on his arm. "You're right, Dad, I should have never left this place," he said as he put his arm around his father's shoulder and turned to the fields. "It is beautiful."

"It is. It is the literal fruit of my labor, and of Pablo and those other guys who help me out. But they wouldn't know what to do without my guidance."

"Of course not, Dad."

John's dad went and sat where John had been sitting. "Everything aside, this will all belong to you one day and that day may not be very far away. I'm a fat fuck who likes to drink. I wake up early and do my thing out in the field, but a lot of the year I'm just sitting on my ass watching this dumbass dog lick itself. What an ability, huh?"

"Very impressive."

"If it were up to your mother, we would have sold all of this a long time ago and moved the hell away from here."

"Why haven't you? Don't you have enough saved up to just call it quits and go?"

"John," said his dad in a resigned voice. "Where are we going to go? This is all I know. I can't leave now. I have to see it through. Whatever *it* is."

He took a long sip of coffee and exhaled, his breath marked in the damp morning air.

"That's true, Dad. To be completely honest with you, I don't want to stay here forever, but I think staying here a while will do me good."

"I agree, son."

The two of them enjoyed each other's company, as the first sun rays hit the tops of the corn.

John's dad stood up from the chair and walked toward a barn that stood at the side of the house. "So, I'll see you at ten then?"

"What's at ten?"

"What do you mean what's at ten? We have a meeting."

Are you fucking kidding me?

"Are you fucking kidding me? Meeting for what?"

"A planning meeting, John."

"Planning?!"

"Yes, planning. Don't sound too excited."

"What are we planning?" asked John in a scared and angry tone.

"What? Do you think we're just going to go willy-nilly up to the fields and start just harvesting whatever piece of corn your dick feels is right? You have to plan. You always plan and make sure you've scoped things out correctly. We need to make sure that Pablo also brought everything that's necessary."

Just when I thought I was out...

EOF

Made in United States
Troutdale, OR
07/31/2023